GOD WHO IS LOVE

Theology and Life Series
1

GOD WHO IS LOVE

in the experience and thought of
Chiara Lubich

Marisa Cerini

New City Press

Published in the United States by New City Press
206 Skillman Avenue, Brooklyn, New York 11211
©1992 New City Press, New York

Translated by Jerry Hearne from the original Italian edition
Dio Amore nell'esperienza e nel pensiero di Chiara Lubich
©1991 Città Nuova, Rome, Italy

Cover design by Nick Cianfarani

Library of Congress Cataloging-in-Publication Data:

Cerini, Marisa.
    [Dio Amore. English]
    God who is love : in the experience and thought of Chiara Lubich / Marisa Cerini.
    p. cm. -- (Theology and life series [Brooklyn, New York, N.Y.])
    Translation of: Dio Amore.
    Includes bibliographical references.
    ISBN 1-56548-004-X : $5.95
    1. Lubich, Chiara, 1920- . 2. God--Love--History of doctrines--20th century. 3. Focolare Movement. I. Title. II. Series.
    BX4705.L792C47   1992
    231'.6--dc20
                                              92-7169

Scriptural quotations are from *The New American Bible*
©1970 Confraternity of Christian Doctrine

Printed in the United States of America

Contents

Preface 7

Introduction 8
  The theological value of Christian experience . 9

Chapter 1: Like a flash of lightning—the discovery
that God is love 11

Chapter 2: Because God is love, he is a Father . . . 20
  God's paternal love 20
  The providence and mercy of the Father . . . 26

Chapter 3: Responding to God-Love by being love . 33
  Believing in love 33
  Responding to Love by loving 38
  To be love 39

Chapter 4: Because God is love, he is Trinity 42
  The Tri-unity of God who is love 45
  The intra-trinitarian dynamism of God-Love . . 48
  The Trinity living in the individual 53
  The Trinity present among those who are
    united in the name of Christ 55

Chapter 5: **Trinitarian love in the workings of the three divine persons** 61
    The Creator 62
    The Redeemer 66
    The Sanctifier 69

Mary—The radiant image of God who is love 73

Abbreviations 75

Notes 77

PREFACE

With this study I have begun to uncover the wealth of wisdom and theological doctrine that the Spirit has entrusted to Chiara Lubich[1] as a gift to pass on to the people of our time.

The central theme of this volume is God-Love in Chiara Lubich's experience and thought. In the light of the gospel message, which is always new, and in the light of the profound teachings of the Fathers of the Church and recent theological reflections, Chiara's contributions emerge in continuation with the most genuine tradition of the Church. At the same time, her experience and thought also convey an authentic novelty that enables her to offer direction and to make an original contribution to modern society's aspirations and its search for meaning in life.

Chiara's charism has thus newly unveiled the face of the living God to great numbers of people and urges them to carry out among all his plan of love: the full unity of everyone with him and with one another.

In an unforgettable encounter in January 1949, this light and life became also for me the illuminating answer to all my aspirations. I immediately felt a call to live it following Chiara. That life and light which has little by little penetrated my whole being and way of living has guided and enlightened this present work.

INTRODUCTION

If we go to the heart of what God has revealed of himself to humanity, looking at the entire content of the scriptures and the spiritual and doctrinal history of the Church, it becomes clear, perhaps today more than ever, that what he wants known of himself is this: that *he, God, is love* (cf. 1 Jn 4:8-16).

We begin therefore examining the reality of God-Love in the extraordinary experience of Chiara Lubich, trying to bring to light its rich theological content. It is an experience of our times that lies at the basis of the spirituality and the vast movement that it has generated.

We intend to introduce and guide a reflection on this fundamental truth of our faith by examining the Word of God and the teaching of the Church, always being attentive to the questions and aspirations of people today.

Our overall objective is to take a look at the unique and entire Christian mystery from many different perspectives which correspond to the fundamental points that define and summarize the spirituality of the Focolare[2] movement. Each perspective will require a separate volume.

This spirituality, like others—"is Christianity itself," "it is the gospel," but seen from the "unity that Jesus asked to the Father for us."[3]

The different points of this spirituality, furthermore, are intrinsically linked with one another, as are the truths of faith which they refer to. Each deepens an aspect of the spirituality, and therefore a truth of faith. At the same time, however, each point embraces and in a certain way contains all the others and, therefore, all the truths of faith.

In this first volume we will look at the entire Christian mystery from the perspective of "God-Love." It is the first point of this spirituality; in its historical development it is its starting point. While being the first point, it embraces and contains, at the same time, the entire spirituality, and therefore our entire faith.[4]

The theological value of Christian experience

The theological value of Christian experience is now widely accepted and since the time of Vatican II (cf. DV 8) it has been rediscovered as a source of theological knowledge or as essential "theological ground."[5]

An authentic Christian experience in fact—which occurs within the realm of faith, therefore within the realm of the Church—enables God, Christ, the Holy Spirit, the Church and other divine realities to be perceived as concrete realities. This experience helps develop a relationship with them and at the same time draws from them practical applications for life.

Such experience engenders, not only on a vital and intuitive level, but also on the intellectual and cognitive, a deeper penetration of the truths of faith and, in particular, their sources—scripture and tradition—which presuppose and lead to that experience. Herein lies its importance for Christian life and for theological knowledge.[6]

The ongoing penetration of the Christian mystery, as a document from the International Theological Commission recently affirmed, "is inspired, sustained, and guided by the action of the Holy Spirit in the Church and in the heart of every Christian. It occurs in the light of faith and receives impetus from the charisms and the witness of those saints which the Spirit of God gives to the Church in a given epoch. Equally growing out of the same context is the prophetic witness of spiritual movements and the interior wisdom deriving from the spiritual experience of laypersons imbued in the Spirit of God" (cf. DV 8).[7]

It is the common conviction of many contemporary theologians that Christian practice and theology must proceed together. "A Church," Schneider observes, "which is founded on 'the apostles and prophets' (Eph 2:20), on ministry and charism . . . cannot but remain fruitfully enriched by the interdependence of theology and sanctity, theological doctrine and 'theology lived.' "[8]

The fact is, as Chenu and others affirm, that spiritualities do express themselves in theological systems, and therefore produce them. "This is where," he concludes, "their interest and greatness lie."[9]

We know, too, that there is an unquestionable connection between Christian experience and theology for the Orthodox theologians. "Theology and mysticism," writes Lossky, "support and complement one another. . . . Therefore, there is no Christian mysticism without theology, but even more so, there is no theology without mysticism." And Evdokimov: "Theology is mysticism and the mystical life is theological, and more than that, it is the apex of theology, theology par excellence."[10]

What has been said thus far holds particularly true, as we shall see, for any approach to that mystery which is the basis and the object both of life and of Christian theology: the mystery of "God who is love, and because he is love, is Trinity."[11]

Chapter 1

LIKE A FLASH OF LIGHTNING
THE DISCOVERY THAT GOD IS LOVE

The beginnings of the spirituality which the Holy Spirit has given life to in Chiara was marked by a strong illumination, like a new revelation, that God is love.

The profound understanding of him that derived from this was for Chiara and for her companions to whom she immediately communicated her intuitions, an entirely new discovery. It was so dazzling as to lead them to a total change of mentality and of life.[1]

But let's go directly to Chiara's own writings, the spring from which we will draw, in all its freshness, the living water of the Word that God wanted to pronounce to the world today through her.

We will begin by citing what she herself related of this first and fundamental illumination when invited to speak on her experience of "God-Love and charity."

Chiara was twenty-three years old. Though a practicing Christian, she was searching for what could satisfy her thirst for truth and how she could live out her ardent desire to maintain an ever vibrant love for God. All the while, she saw with regret that the Christianity of her time too often appeared emptied of its vitality and its effectiveness:

> In the midst of all kinds of inconsistencies and contradictions, God was drawing me to himself. At a moment when the way we Christians were living deeply distressed me, he manifested himself.
> Exactly when, I do not know. His subtle light

entered in and enlightened me. As it enwrapped my soul, it did not suppress my former ideas, but slowly replaced them with new ones.

One fact I recall. I was still in school. A priest who was passing through . . . wanted to have a word with me. He asked me to offer up an hour of my day for his intentions. I answered: "Why not the entire day?" Struck by such youthful generosity . . . he told me: "Remember that God loves you immensely."

This was the blinding light.

"God loves me immensely." "God loves me immensely."

I told it to my companions: God loves you immensely. God loves us immensely.

Since that moment I see God present everywhere with his love: in daytime, during the night, in my enthusiasm, in my resolutions, in events that are joyful and comforting, in situations that prove to be sad, awkward, or difficult.

He is always there, he is present everywhere, and he explains things to me. What does he explain? *That everything is love.* All that I am and all that regards me. All that we are and all that regards us. That I am his child and he is my Father. That nothing escapes his love, not even the mistakes I make, because *he permits them*; that his love envelops Christians like myself, that it embraces the Church, the world, and the entire universe.

And he sustains me and opens my eyes to see everything and everyone, equally so, as expressions of his love.

The conversion has come about. The "novelty" has flashed through my mind: I know who God is. God is love.

God is love.

We are aware of it. We are most deeply convinced of it. Everything in our life has changed. A smile arises continually on our faces, all through the hardships of war, in our detachments, when we find ourselves under the bombardments, even in our proximity to death.[2] Everything is an expression of God's love.

As though he were planting a seed in the ground, he places within our hearts this new faith in his love.

This is our great discovery, our immense discovery. The world around us is unaware of it. I have communicated the news to everyone I can: to my mother, my father, my sisters, my brother, my friends.

We believe in love. This is our new life. For this reason we have expressed our desire—should we die in the war—to be buried in a single tomb with the words that express our being, written as our name: "And we have believed in love" (cf. 1 Jn 4:16).[3]

Chiara's personal letters during those years communicate the overwhelming discovery of this reality, and attest to the infusion of "light" and of "fire" with which God-Love became present in her life.

In June 1944 she wrote:

You have been blinded with me by the fiery brilliance of an Ideal that exceeds all things and contains all:

by the infinite love of God!

It is he, he, my God and your God, who has established a bond between us that is stronger than death. . . .

It is Love who has called us to love!

It is Love who has spoken in the depths of our hearts and has told us:

13

"Look around you. Everything in the world passes away. Every day sees its evening, and how quickly each evening comes. . . . *Love that which does not die! Love the one who is love!"*

Love, love, love! People are created to love.

Yes, there is suffering in the world, but for the one who loves, suffering is nothing; even martyrdom is a song! Even the cross is a song. God is love! Every suffering is a sure test of love, its unmistakable divine seal. . . .

Therefore: we cannot let any sorrow in our lives go by without accepting it and desiring it, so as to prove to God, who is infinite love, our own little but steadfast love!

Let's leave our hearts with just one desire: to love!

Let's let our minds be intent on confronting our every thought with the infinite and immense love of God.[4]

"We must not become attached to anything," she writes in another letter, "because everything passes away. Only God, who is love, can light a flame within us that will last the duration of this life and for all eternity."[5]

This early experience of Chiara already contains the power of new life and a very intense light of wisdom. From it emerge, with extraordinary splendor and vitality, the fundamental aspects that God manifests of himself as love throughout all of revelation: that the infinite, the absolute, enters into a relationship of love with the finite. They are the aspects upon which the Church's theological thought has developed.

God—"who is the inexpressible one, the ineffable, the infinite, the eternal"[6]—manifests himself to Chiara. by revealing his immense love, his fatherhood, his providence that embraces everyone and everything. He reveals as well his presence of love in every place and event, and in this love the answer to everything, even to what pertains to suffering and to error. And this very act of manifesting himself is itself an expression of his love. It *is* love. It is the gift of himself. Having come to this experience, through a special action of grace, Chiara receives a completely new awareness of him. She now "knows" who God is: God is love. Having discovered in her own personal life and in the history of humanity the way God acts—a way which is all love—she understands that God's very being is love.

Thus, according to the divine pedagogy common to every form of revelation, which on the part of God is always a communication and gift of himself, the Holy Spirit raised to life and made concrete[7] in Chiara and in her companions the central truth of the Christian mystery: "God is love" (1 Jn 4:8-16).

God is love. It is the affirmation that the apostle John makes at the culminating point of the age-old journey of revelation, throughout which God had constantly demonstrated his love to humankind. Love is the profound meaning of all his interventions in the history of Israel, from the call of Abraham to the Sinai Covenant, from his constant presence in the midst of his people to his continual regathering them after their every fall.

What is more, love is the purpose of the creative action itself, out of which, from nothing, God calls human beings into existence and at the same time elevates them to the most intimate communion with him. The love of God, evidenced by the prophets in its greatness, its intensity, and its steadfastness, reaches the apex of communication in the gift of the Son and the Spirit. The only Son, "who is in the bosom of the Father" (Jn 1:18, RSV), having become a man, manifests this love in the midst of human beings throughout his life. He does so even to his death on the cross, so "that we might have life" (1 Jn 4:9). The Spirit, through whom "the love of God has been poured out into our hearts" (Rom 5:5), continues to attest to this.

John is the disciple Jesus loved, the eyewitness of this love, the theologian of charity. In his affirmation "God is love," he expresses with extreme conciseness and unsurpassable clarity "the outcome of what he contemplated in the numerous manifestations of God's love throughout the course of history, which is a history of salvation,"[8] up to the fullness of time, when in Christ he made his love visible and tangible to the utmost degree (cf. 1 Jn 4:9).

God, in fact, reveals to humanity who he is through what he does.

If his love is the ultimate purpose of his interaction with humanity, of the very revelation of himself, and of the end—the full sharing of humanity in his life—of his action and self-revelation, and it is a love without measure and beyond comparison, it means that it is the most specific characteristic of his being; it is what essentially constitutes his being. Love is his nature. Love is the name of the living God.[9]

When revealing himself to Moses, he told him that he was "the one who is" (cf. Ex 3:14). This expression, which in Hebrew is dynamic in significance and means "the one who is there," always projected toward the good of the other, already contains in itself, though implicit, the indication that his being is love.

At the completion of the era of revelation the apostle John will twice declare in his letter that "God is love" (1 Jn 4:8-16).

In our present time, Pope John Paul II, in developing a profound theological synthesis explaining the unity of what had been revealed, asserted: "God is love. *This is the name of the one who is.*"¹⁰

This Christian declaration, radically surpassing the image of a God relegated to an insurmountable distance from the world and its people, manifests a new—the true—face of God. It is that of a "God," Kasper writes, "whose essence is life and love, and for this reason can be the God of human beings and the God of history." From this he derives then "that love is the ultimate purpose of every reality." "This Christian conception of reality," Kasper observes, "is so revolutionary in interpreting what is real, that it is difficult to imagine something greater."¹¹

This is the face of God newly revealed to Chiara in a moment in history when such an awareness was no longer present in the conscience of Christians, and therefore in their way of thinking and acting. Instead, an atheistic and secularized vision was making ever greater headway.

For this reason Chiara says: "The 'novelty' flashed through my mind," and on another occasion, "it was an absolute novelty for us."¹² It was such a novelty that it effected in the first Focolarine a turn around, a "conversion," as she says, in their way of seeing the world and history: "everything is love." Consequently, it influenced the way they lived.

"God-Love," Chiara herself will explain, "not a God who is distant, immovable and inaccessible to people. God-Love who comes to meet every person in thousands of ways...." God-Love: "love in himself, love for all of his creation."¹³

It is very meaningful, furthermore, that a young girl, after receiving a manifestation of God's personal love for her—"God loves you ..." "God loves me immensely"—

became convinced of it and communicated to others that God loves each and every one immensely. This is a sign that God "chose" her to make her an instrument of his, in view of carrying out a plan whose universal dimension could already be foreseen. He enveloped her in his light so that she might pass it on; he communicated to her that his being is love. Together with this gift she was also given an irrepressible impetus to bear witness to and reveal this love to others.

Besides the gift of the "immense discovery" of God-Love, Chiara recognizes another gift from him: the "entirely new faith in him as love" which arose in her heart and in the hearts of her companions. This new faith was the light and inner drive which made them respond to God's love, to the relationship that he as a Father established with them, with the trust and joy typical of the "children" of the gospel.

This illumination that filled their entire being—since their hearts and minds were called to "perennially confront everything with God's infinite love" and so to be its reflection—paved the way for the radicality of their response of love.

Chiara affirms, "We would not have had any meaning in the world if we were not a little flame of this infinite fire: love that responds to Love."[14]

The profound theological value of this total and conscious response is evident. Scheffczyk writes, "since the love of God is none other than the sharing of his life with humanity, the response of love on the part of the latter is contained in the essence of the act with which God gives of himself." "Even though put into action by the person's free will, [the response] is caused and produced by divine love."[15]

Thus, against the dramatic background of the war, which showed all things to be precarious and transitory—

"everything passes away," "everything dies"—God-Love emerged as the most real and true reality of all realities. Chiara and her first companions chose him as the everything of their lives, with "the most ardent desire to be faithful to him their entire lives as the saints were. God, therefore, and nothing else."[16]

The shining incarnation of this new Ideal[17] in their lives, the clarity and the depth with which they express and communicate it has an immediate influence on those who come—and on those who will come—into close contact with this way of life.

God-Love, therefore, was the starting point of the newly born spirituality of the Focolare. While springing forth from the deepest roots of Christian tradition, the spirituality also showed itself early on to be rich in a genuine *novelty* of life and doctrine for Christianity and for the world of today.

The Church, on various occasions, has affirmed that a spirituality is the fruit of a charism. Tillard defines a charism as having "the capability of reading into—with new understanding—the entire Christian mystery in the light of one of its essential aspects."[18] And Rahner points out that a charism always blossoms in the Church as essentially new, yet in mysterious continuity with all that precedes it in the Church. At the same time it engrafts itself to the Church[19] because it belongs to the free and unforeseeable action of the Spirit who continually renews the Church and leads it toward the fullness of truth (cf. Jn 16:23).

Chapter 2
BECAUSE GOD IS LOVE, HE IS A FATHER

In this revealing experience of God as love, Chiara discovered in a deeply new way his being a Father to her and her being a child of his. Along with her, Chiara's companions had the same experience. They all immediately felt a relationship with him which was previously unknown. Enveloped and sustained by his paternal love, though surrounded by the hardships of war, they lived in trust, in security, in light and in peace.[1]

"The life we lived before," Chiara will say, "though rich in solid faith and practice, appears darkened, as though we were living as orphans.

"Now everything is new. 'God is love' (1 Jn 4:8). And, because he is love, he is Father."[2]

From that moment on, the intimate and concrete relationship initiated with him will no longer be interrupted. Chiara, her companions, and, as time goes on, all those who follow their way of life discover him as a Father. Certain of his timely interventions, they turn to him every day as his children.

God's paternal love

In many of her writings, Chiara testifies to a repeated unfolding in her life of the inexpressible and mysterious reality of the Father. It is her desire to make this relationship more known and more experienced, for it is the "novelty" that Jesus reveals, the pivotal element in the "good news."

God—who is and remains Lord, and to whose will everything is submitted (cf. Mt 7:21)—is the Father who is in heaven (cf. Mt 6:9), who makes the sun shine on the good and on the bad alike, and makes the rain fall on the just and on the unjust (cf. Mt 5:45), who watches over all (cf. Mt 6:26-32); and who, through Jesus, instructs us and authorizes us to call him Father. This is who God is for humankind. This is the name with which he, who is love, can and wishes to be invoked: Father, "Our Father" (Mt 6:9).

The gospel sentence "and pray to your Father . . ." (Mt 6:6) inspires Chiara to put into writing words of rare beauty, of profound theological value. She discloses the experience of her relationship with the Father, which these very words revive for her. Presenting herself to him, she offers her entire self to her Creator "just as she is," and she feels received by him as a daughter. In Jesus she recognizes the one who revealed him and gave him to us. In the Spirit she finds the one who makes concrete this revelation and gift to the point of placing on our lips the word "Abba, Father!"—a word through which we immerse ourselves in him, in his kingdom, the kingdom of intra-trinitarian love.

Jesus, so this is how you reveal it! This is how you announce the reality that I have a Father!

A Father! The Father! . . .

That a Father exists who thinks of me is something inexpressible.

And Jesus, even before dying, before redeeming us and giving us the Father, spoke of him as though he were already so known.

But it is not known, Jesus, what you say! The Good News is such a novelty that it is always new!

We have a Father! I have a Father!

Father! Our Father . . .

Who can be richer than we are, than I am?
Father, here I am in the privacy of my room. I do not feel the need to explain or to analyze myself in order to present myself before you.
I feel only the need to give myself entirely to you just as I am. . . .
And I am certain that you, in secret, listen, understand and accept me as your daughter.
Oh! Who is it who revealed to me on this blessed day this reality of yours that so pertains to my life? It must certainly be the Holy Spirit. He is the one who places on our lips the word "Abba, Father!" He places this same word within the soul, which, by immersing itself in it, finds his kingdom, where the soul is looked upon and loved just as it is.[3]

In a more recent writing of hers which shows an intimate correlation between theological knowledge and sapiential penetration into mystery, Chiara brings to light the basis of this divine relationship between Father and child, which every person is called to.

In fact, at the root of the revelation and of the gift of the Father that Jesus gave to us by virtue of the Holy Spirit, there is an ontological reality; that is, the reality unique and belonging only to him, of being the Son of this Father.

God, our Father who is in heaven, allows a glimpse of the abysmal depths and fruitfulness of his being Father, in the person and the historical life of his incarnate Son. In a human and visible nature, Jesus is "the image of the Invisible God" (Col 1:15), "the radiance of God's glory and the exact representation of his being" (Heb 1:3, RSV), to the point of being able to say of himself: "whoever has seen me has seen the Father" (Jn 14:9).

The gospels portray, in a crescendo of affirmations,

the reciprocity of knowlege, of love, and of life which joins the Son to the Father in an incomparable unity of being and of will: "No one knows the Son but the Father, and no one knows the Father but the Son" (Mt 11:27); "All that belongs to me is yours, and all that belongs to you is mine" (Jn 17:10); "The Father and I are one" (Jn 10:30).

Jesus, "the Son that he loves" (Col 1:13, NJB) and sent by his love to save the world (cf. Jn 3:16-18), is the only Son of God (cf. Jn 1:14-18), his beloved Son, upon whom his favor rests, as the Father from heaven declares (cf. Mk 9:7 and Mt 3:17). He is the one whom the Father loved "before the world began" (Jn 17:24).

Jesus orients his entire life toward the Father. He lives in a very special and personal relationship with him, in such full accord with his will and in the unshakable certainty of his love that when turning to him in prayer he not only calls him "Father," or "my Father" (Mt 11:25; Lk 10:21; Mt 26:39-42), but "Abba" (Mk 14:36).

Calling him in this way, which really means "Dad," and which appears totally new in the Judaic world as an invocation to God, Jesus expresses the unique trust and profound intimacy that he has with the Father. Thus he reveals, by coming to live in human history, the eternal relationship that he has with him within the Trinity: that being God's Son is his very nature.[4]

In referring to this same invocation, Chiara, in her writing, shows that the intra-trinitarian relationship of Jesus with the Father is the basis for the possibility given also to us to be introduced as sons and daughters—in the Son, through the Holy Spirit—into the bosom of the Trinity.

Chiara writes:

> Jesus prayed; he prayed to the Father. He called the Father "Abba," which means "Dad," the one

whom he turned to with infinite trust and boundless love. He prayed to him from the bosom of the Trinity, where he is the second divine person. It was precisely through this very special prayer that he revealed to the world who he really was: the Son of God.

However, since he came to earth for us, it was not enough for him to be alone in this privileged condition of prayer. By dying for us and by redeeming us, he made us children of God, his own brothers and sisters. By means of the Holy Spirit he provided the possibility also for us to be introduced into the heart of the Trinity, through him, with him, and in him. In so doing, we too can now repeat the same divine invocation: "Abba, Father!" (cf. Mk 14:36 and Rom 8:15), "Dad, my Dad, our Dad," with everything that this implies: the certainty of his protection, our confidence and trustful surrender to his love, divine consolation, strength, and ardor, that ardor that is born in the heart of one who is certain of being loved. . . .

This is what Christian prayer is; it is an extraordinary form of prayer. . . . Here we enter into the very heart of God.[5]

In this page Chiara recalls and forms into a luminous synthesis various heights of Christian mystery, from the intra-trinitarian generation of the eternal Son to the gift of divine sonship for all people. She draws attention to this gift as being a lofty vocation.

From all eternity, the Father, in loving the Son, generates him and in turn is loved by him in the steadfastness of the same love, in the Holy Spirit, love which is hypostatic. It is in this eternal act that God expresses his being Father in its essential and perfect dimension. It is his being Father in the internal life of the Trinity that precedes and is the basis for his paternity toward humanity.

In fact, he has not only called the people of the earth into existence, but he also guides them toward the completion of a purpose that lies already in the Word, in the Son, before the creation of the world itself. The Son, as the God-Man, is present from all eternity in the divine plan as the true and complete plan of God for humankind. Therefore, in the Word, which is in the bosom of the Father, there is the starting point, so to say, and the ultimate end of all divine creative action.[6]

"In the beginning was the Word," John writes, ". . . and the Word was God. He was present to God in the beginning. Through him all things came into being" (Jn 1:1-3). Constantly and completely turned toward the Word, the Father contemplates his plan, and in a new effusion of love and of life, through the Word and his Spirit, he freely unfolds this plan in history.

Paul, on his part, ascertains that "all were created through him and for him . . . everything continues in being in him" who "is before all else that is" (Col 1:16-17). He thus shows Christ to be the eternal and vital origin, mediator, and vertex of all creation.

Thus the whole of humanity therefore—and in humanity the cosmos—eternally present in the Word in the form of a plan, created through him and re-created by means of his redemptive incarnation, will come "together under Christ, as head" (cf. Eph 1:10) and will be definitively assumed into the eternal act of the generation of the Son by the Father, in the heart of the Trinity.

It is above all, therefore, in the incarnate Son, in the God-Man, that the Father joins humanity to himself in an immediate and direct paternal relationship; it is above all in the incarnate Son that humanity responds with an equally immediate and direct filial relationship.

Through the incarnate Son, men and women redeemed by him, made "new creatures" through the gift of the Spirit, and thus made "sharers of the divine nature" (2 Pt 1:4), become, in an adoption of grace, children of God. This causes John to exclaim: "See what love the Father has bestowed on us in letting us be called children of God! Yet that is what we are" (1 Jn 3:1).[7]

Paul, in illustrating this on various occasions, attests to the reality of our divine sonship. As Bouyer notes, having become with Christ "one being through baptism (cf. Rom 6), in which we live of his life, death, and resurrection, and nourished with his body in the eucharist to the extent of becoming and of being members of this body" (cf. 1 Cor 11:12), we have been established as sons and daughters in the Son, "coheirs of what pertains to the one 'inheritance' of the Father (cf. Rom 8:17 and Gal 4:7), of all that he is and of all that he has."[8]

Therefore the very same reciprocity of love, of knowledge, and of life that joins the Son to the Father in the Spirit, becomes established—as Chiara notes—also between the Father and ourselves. We can already in this life turn to him in the same filial relationship and call upon him with the same invocation of Jesus: "Abba" (cf. Rom 8:15 and Gal 4:6).

The providence and mercy of the Father

God, who manifests his paternal love in countless ways, led Chiara to discover—as she always testifies herself—that behind everything and everyone, behind any joyful or painful circumstance of life, he who is love is there. He is present with his providence, which works all things to the good for those who love him. All that happens, therefore, is seen as willed or permitted by him. This gives her a deep conviction about Jesus' words: "As for you, every hair on your head has been counted" (Mt 10:30).[9]

Chiara, in reference to these striking and consoling words of the gospel, writes:

> We need to feel looked upon and *loved* by God. We need to know that every one of our prayers of offering or thanksgiving, every word we pronounce as a result of listening to his voice, every move we make, every event . . . whether sad, joyful or indifferent, every sickness, everything, everything, everything, from the things we consider important to our smallest actions, thoughts, and sentiments, are looked upon by God. To know this comforts us, makes us feel that we are in company, even when we are alone, and in company above all with the only one who is truly important to us.[10]

Chiara sees how the entire history of the Focolare was and is a testimony to this continual presence and providence of the Father. He is present in each moment in the same way as in his extraordinary interventions. He faithfully keeps his gospel promises, always in surprising ways, "as 'these other things will be given you besides,' which punctually arrive for having sought his kingdom; and as the 'hundred times more' that heaven sends for having put aside, at least spiritually, all things for Jesus" (cf. Lk 12:31 and Mt 19:29).[11] All these things are cause for joy because they become tangible signs of the invisible but concrete love of the Father. Everything is seen in the light of the gospel.

There was one particular circumstance in which a unique intervention of providence prompted Chiara to say, "God, who thinks of the birds of the air and the lilies of the field, thinks also of his children. We too could write the gospel, at least in view of our experience of this divine adventure between father and children."[12]

So constant is this reality a part of the life of the Focolare that it has even found a place in its written statutes, along with the corresponding passage of the gospel.

> The members of the Work of Mary entrust themselves to God's providence, who provides for the needs of those who seek his kingdom. They are committed, in fact, to putting into practice Jesus' words: "Look at the birds in the sky. They do not sow or reap, they gather nothing into barns; yet your heavenly Father feeds them. Are not you more important than they?" (Mt 6:26). "Stop worrying, then, over questions like, 'What are we to eat, or what are we to drink, or what are we to wear?' The unbelievers are always running after these things. Your heavenly Father knows all that you need. Seek first his kingship over you, his way of holiness, and all these things will be given you besides' (Mt 6:31-33)."[13]

God, therefore, is Father: a Father who watches over the life of each and every person and over the whole of humanity as well.

But his paternal love, which provides for our needs to the smallest detail, manages to fill even the deepest gaps, those that are a result of sin. His love becomes mercy.

Mercy is the full expression of God's love; he is the "Father of mercies" (2 Cor 1:3). This dimension of his love is so essential and inalienable that John Paul II recognizes mercy as the "second name" of his love and, "at the same time, the specific manner in which love is revealed and effected vis-à-vis the reality of the evil that is in the world, affecting and besieging man."[14]

It is, in fact, in the light of God's merciful love that his entire plan of salvation can be explained, a plan which, since the very beginning, has been interwoven in the history of humanity (cf. Sir 18:10-12) and in the lives of individuals (cf. Ps 51 and 2 Sm 24:14). Both are marked by repeated moments of falling away from him, to which he responds with his forgiveness and his faithfulness. It is in virtue of this love that is always reaching down that he makes his covenant with human beings. Those who before were "not his people" he makes his people, those who were "unloved" he makes the loved ones in mercy (cf. Hos 1:6-9 and 2:21-23).

The New Testament will unfold all the different tones of the Father's merciful love: from his turning toward those whom the world considered to be mere children (cf. Mt 11:25), to his attention to the needy (cf. Mt 6:32), to his great concern for the oppressed (cf. Lk 4:18-19), and even to his meeting with sinners, whether searching for them (cf. Lk 15:4-7) or confidently awaiting them in order to rejoice and happily welcome their return (cf. Lk 15:11-32).[15]

Mercy, therefore, speaks of all the gratuitousness and the boundlessness of God's love, who makes the first move toward humankind in order to offer his assistance and forgiveness. And more than that: "God," John writes, "so loved the world that he gave his only Son, that whoever believes in him may not die but may have eternal life" (Jn 3:16). St. Paul, in describing the unfathomable measure of this love, writes, "While we were still sinners, Christ died for us" (Rom 5:8), so that "when we were dead through our sins," we might "be brought back to life" with him (cf. Eph 2:4-5).

This is the mystery of the redemptive incarnation in

which the mercy of God reaches down to the world and completely shares in the human condition.

The Son, in becoming man, not only took on our finite nature, but he took upon himself our wretchedness; he made himself "sin," in the eyes of the Father, "for us" (cf. 2 Cor 5:21 and Gal 3:13). Thus he measured, in the depth of his being, the entire weight of our distance from the father (cf. Mk 15:34), so as to offer to him, through his death, a proportional gift—the total gift of himself, the God-Man. This gift of himself, cancelled out every sin of ours and, in completely closing the gap of our distance from the Father, opened up for us, forever, our communion with God (cf. Heb 2:9-10).

In a wonderful synthesis, Chiara depicts the dynamics of this gift of love of the Father and of the Son for us, wherein the fullness of divine mercy is revealed. The Father, she writes, gives the Son and the Son gives the Father, his mother, and himself "for us," in order to make us capable of receiving "the greatest good a person could ever imagine: his very life." Thus mercy shows itself as it truly is and continues to be in history: the "transforming and creative power" of God's love which gives back to humankind its true worth and, by regenerating in it "the new creation," restores to humankind the dignity of being God's children.[16]

Humanity, in its turn, redeemed and introduced into the fullness of the invigorating life of the Father, of the Son, and of the Holy Spirit, and, for the very same reason, made sharer of God's merciful movement of love, is called to actively live of this love. Humanity is called to put this into practice with every neighbor, in imitation of the Father (cf. Lk 6:36) and of his perfect image, Christ, who "has come to search out and save what was lost" (Lk 19:10).

There is a page in Chiara's writings that offers a clear example of this astonishing analogy between the ways of God, all-merciful love, and the ways of those who, made similar to Christ through the experience of suffering transformed into love, go out to encounter the hardships of others in order to share in and to alleviate them.

"After experiencing the unique value of suffering," Chiara writes, "after believing in the economy of the cross and seeing its beneficial effects, the moment comes when God shows something in a new and higher form which is worth even more than suffering. *It is love for others in the form of mercy*, love which opens heart and arms to the unfortunate, to the needy, to those torn by life's adversities, to repentant sinners.

'It is a love that knows how to welcome back the neighbor who has gone astray—whether this is a friend, a brother, a sister or a stranger—and it forgives this person an infinite number of times. It is a love that rejoices more over a sinner who repents than over a thousand righteous people. It lends intelligence and possessions to God so that the prodigal son may be shown the happiness caused by his return.

'It is a love that does not measure and will not be measured," a love that is "abundant," "universal," "active," moved by "sentiments which resemble those of Jesus," which bring to one's lips his same divine words: "I feel sorry for all these people" (Mt 15:32, NJB).

"Mercy is charity's highest form of expression, the attribute which fulfills it."[17]

This is how the children of God live. They resemble him in all things, and make the Father's plan of salvation visible in each historical moment, thus renewing it for all people. This salvific plan was completed by Christ once and for all (cf. Heb 10:10). Maximus the Confessor writes: "A person will be a resemblance of God if, in imitating God's love for all, he or she heals in a divine way the sufferings of the unfortunate and through practice and example gives a living proof of the saving providence of God."[18]

Chapter 3
RESPONDING TO GOD-LOVE BY BEING LOVE

God reveals and communicates himself to humanity with expressions that are typical of his love—his paternity, his active presence in history, his power that liberates. Humanity is called to respond to him by believing and entrusting itself to his love, to love him in return to the point of becoming similar to him, to becoming love as he is love.

Believing in love

In one of Chiara's writings we have read that right from the very beginning God had "deposited" in her heart and in the hearts of the first Focolarine an "entirely new faith in him as love," the striking conviction that God loved each and every one of them in an immense way.

"It is an exalting faith," Chiara writes, "that strengthens and uplifts us." "From that moment on, this faith in God's love for us, his love for each and for everyone, for all of humanity, enlightened our entire lives."[1]

It is a faith that gives a new vision and understanding to all of life. Since God is love, persons and things, circumstances and events, are all seen as belonging to a single universal design which tells of his love.

If God is love, the logical consequence would be to place our entire trust in him.

Chiara affirms that each and every one of us can

entrust ourselves to him, "sure of being understood, comforted, helped and known by him to the very core of our being."[2] We can ask him to safeguard this faith. "Lord," she writes, "keep me in your love. Do not let me live even a moment without being aware, feeling and knowing through faith, or even through experience, that you love me, that you love all of us."[3]

This faith in love, which is an acceptance and a profession of the revealed truth and, at the same time, a total and free assent of the mind and an adherence of one's entire being, comes to determine for those who live it, the fundamental orientation of their life. It brings about a personal and dynamic relationship with God[4] that so greatly marks one's personality as to become its predominant trait. Chiara urges that "believing in love and acting accordingly must become your identity."[5]

Thus, in the centuries-long course of Christian spirituality, a new type of follower of Christ stands out. It is one whose being is shaped by a faith in Love, which in Christ is resplendent and operative in all its ontological and existential transforming power.

Chiara draws an original parallel using the image of the vital relationship of father and child. She delineates the essential characteristics of this new type of Christian, the "child" of the gospel who is fully aware that he or she is a child of a heavenly Father, a child who recognizes and loves the Father as he or she is known and loved by him.

Children as these, in Chiara's description, have complete trust in God. Totally abandoned to him, they are certain that everything that happens is willed or permitted by him for their good. They imitate their Father. Since the Father "loves because he is love," they too, being his children, love to the point of being able to be unmistakably defined as "those who love." They live their earthly lives immersed in the supernatural, in that kingdom of God which is already among us now through the presence of Jesus in the midst of those who love one another (cf. Mt 18:20). They do not see circumstances only in their exterior forms and chronological sequences; they also "know how to read the signs of the times." They recognize the plan of God that lies behind all things. They marvel at the Father's interventions, at his providence that is so timely and concrete. They are joyful and innocent, because they have been "made virgin," "made immaculate" by love;[6] they are "detached from all things and from life itself." Just as children cannot learn to speak on their own, so too, the children of the gospel "are taught the word, the word of God, by the Father, and are 'all word of God.' " Finally, in a way similar to the children who resemble not only their father, but also their mother, these children resemble not only their Father, but also Mary, their mother.[7]

But, to believe in God's love, as Chiara observes, means to believe that God is love also in the obscure experience of suffering.

"In the difficult moments of my life," she writes, "I have seen that there is one single idea that rules my soul and whose presence is like a seal of fire: everything is love. Why? Because God is love."[8]

She continues, "when our faith undergoes a screening test, when, through a series of disturbing circumstances, one has the impression of being no longer loved by God and feels the sensation of having no worth, it is the time to struggle to regain faith in love. God will intervene and we will see the fruits of the trials we have overcome. 'For when I am powerless, it is then that I am strong' (2 Cor 12:10). Therefore, also in moments of extreme weakness, when they are lived as God's will and because we believe in his love, we can experience the surprising inner strength of our true being, which is simple and one, and which shares in the life and the power of that Being which created us, who himself is love and is one."[9]

Chiara affirms that "God will not hold back [his] grace from us even in our most tragic moments.... Let's always and in every circumstance believe in love, in that love which embraces, as a single arch, life on earth and life eternal."[10]

Scripture says, "cast all your cares on him because he cares for you" (1 Pt 5:7).

"The fact is," Chiara comments, "God is a Father and wants his children to be happy. This is why he took upon himself all their trials. God is love and wants his children to be love," free, therefore, from all those worries and concerns which "are obstacles to love."[11]

The experience lived of such faith in love clearly shows what immense possibilities could be opened on ever wider scales if our belief in the Father's love were to become unshakable, and if extended portions of humanity were to come to believe.

It is this universal vision of faith in God-Love which Chiara expresses in the texts that follow.

> If God came down from heaven to earth for us,
> there is no doubt that he loves us.
> And when we know someone loves us,
> even more, when we know God himself loves us,
> everything becomes easier for us on earth,
> everything becomes more understandable.
> Behind life's obscurities
> we can discover his loving hand,
> a purpose often unknown to us,
> but a purpose of love.
> Everything becomes more bearable.
> And everything is much more pervaded with joy,
> should joy be already present.

Behind the delicate traces of life . . .
lies a Father's providence.
Everything becomes possible.
If we believe, if we believe in a God who loves us,
every impossibility can shatter,
even the impossibility so evident at times
that our cradle, the planet that houses us,
lives in peace.
Yes, everything is possible.
What is more, if the All-Powerful came among us,
our faith can reach even greater heights.
We can come to believe,
if we hope for it and ask for it with all our hearts,
that the world may begin its road to unity:
to unity among generations,
among social classes, among races,
among Christians centuries-divided,
among the faithful of different religions,
among all peoples.[12]

We must open the eyes of as many of our brothers and sisters as possible so that they might see and discover the fortune they possess, often without knowing it. They are not alone on this earth. Love is here. They have a Father who does not abandon his children to their own way, but he wants to accompany them, to look after and assist them. He is a Father who does not overburden the shoulders of others, but he is the first to carry their load. . . . He does not leave the renewal of society to the initiative of men and women alone, but he is the first to assume responsibility for it. Everyone must know this and go to him certain that nothing is impossible to him.[13]

Responding to Love by loving

The revelation that God makes of himself as love sparks in the depths of the soul not only an unshakable faith in his immense and personal love, but also an irresistible impulse, as Chiara's experience attests, "to love him with all of one's heart, soul, strength and will" (cf. Lk 10:27).

Chiara recalls that "the dignity to which he raised us seemed to us so sublime, and the possibility to love him in return seemed so high and undeserved that we used to repeat: 'It's not that we should say: we must love God, but rather: Oh, that we can love you, Lord . . . that we can love you with this little heart of ours!' "[14]

We find a reflection of this intense love for God in a letter that dates back to the early times.

> I love God and desire to love him as he was never loved before. I labor to make him loved.
>
> Everything else that happens in my life does not phase me. I have but one desire, one passion: that Love might be loved.
>
> I feel my powerlessness, but I surrender it to God. I base everything on an unshakable faith: . . . I believe that God loves me, and in the name of this love I ask of my own life and of the lives of those who walk in my Ideal great things, worthy of those who know they are loved by God.[15]

And to love God means to do his will, which itself is love and which says that we should love everyone, and love one another. Here begins the commitment to "live and to work for an invasion of love in the world" in order to contribute "to the fulfillment of that 'civilization of love' called for, not without a prophetic vision we think, by Pope Paul VI and by Pope John Paul II."[16]

"God-Love," Chiara affirms, *"to believe in his love and to respond to his love by loving* are the great imperatives of today. *"They are the essentials* that today's generation awaits."[17]

To be love

The one who loves "abides in God" (1 Jn 4:16), in God who is love, shares in his very life, in his divine fruitfulness,[18] and radiates his presence in the world. This person radiates "God, who must shine through our minds, our hearts, our faces, our words, our actions, our silence, our living, our dying, our presence after our departure from this earth, where we can and we must leave behind a luminous streak of his presence, of him present in us, amidst the constructions and the ruins of the world, whether it is thriving or collapsing, in the praise or in the vanity of all things, clearing everything away to make room for everything, for the only one, for *love.*"[19]

However, in order to bear witness to him in this way, we must—as Chiara often says—"never stop loving for a moment." More than that, we must "be Love." "We must shine," as she says using a very effective image, "like little suns next to the sun."[20] In this way, "we are."[21] This is how we live as children of the one who is love. This is the reality which Chiara, with great depth and sublime theological teaching, brings so well to light.

What does God want from us? If God is love, if God is like the sun and like the light, he wants us, as his children, to be little suns, little lights. In a way similar to Christ . . . the Son of God and the incarnate sun, he wants us to be little Christs. In a way similar to Mary, who was another Christ and a little sun, he wants us to be other Marys. God wants us to be perfect in love, because he himself is love, and we are the children of Love.

God wants us to bring to completion in ourselves the immense reality that Jesus expressed in the terms: "You are gods" (Jn 10:34). A Christian is another Christ in Christ, God in God.

Therefore, for those who see or deal with us, it must be as though they are dealing with God. They must almost be able to touch God with their own hands, a God by participation, but a God just the same, a God who is love.

If we are perfect in all the nuances of love that the Holy Spirit has placed in our hearts, and if this love spreads to others, if it draws our soul into a relationship with God, since charity brings us to union with him and with our neighbors, *then we are our true selves*.... God wants us to be little "Saviors," little Christs, little suns, little God-Loves.[22]

It is, therefore, by being Love, "little God-Loves," that we can respond as children to God who is love.

If love, in fact, is God's very being, it is also the being of the people he created. God shares his love with them in the very act in which he makes them part of his own personal being, so that they might be love as he is love.[23] Therefore, by being perfect in the love which God with new fullness deposits in their hearts through the Spirit, men and women find fulfillment according to the divine plan. The human person thus becomes "another Christ in Christ" and lives as a son or daughter in the Son in full communion with the Father.

"In other terms," as the exegete Spicq affirms in his comprehensive study of agape in the New Testament, "agape establishes a communion of nature and of life between the 'one who is generated' and his divine Father; and it is through 'the experience' of agape . . . that the believer becomes what God is."[24] This is where humanity's lofty vocation reaches its completion. The Fathers of the Church expressed this vocation in daring, but real terms. They spoke of "deification," of the "divinization" of the human person, which is brought about in the individual through a life of charity and in virtue of the inexpressible love of God, which is his pure gift. Maximus the Confessor wrote, "The one who is fortified by charity transposes oneself through God in God. God created us . . . so that we might become sharers in the divine nature and that we might enter into his eternity, that we might appear similar to him, having been deified through grace."[25]

Chapter 4
BECAUSE GOD IS LOVE, HE IS TRINITY

Having manifested himself as love, therefore, God showed that he not only loves men and women in infinite measure, but that in the intimate nature of his being, he *is* love; he is agape.[1]

The agape-love of God, as God himself reveals "by deeds and words" (DV 2: F, 751) throughout salvation history to its culmination in Christ's death and resurrection, and as the Church testifies and believers can experience in their own lives—is a gift of himself. It is a love that is unconditional, freely given, and absolute. God is the first to love (cf. 1 Jn 4:19). His love is a creator's love. He loves and creates the value of the being which is loved; he re-creates it. Therefore, in his eyes the human person no longer exists as a sinner alone, but has become a "new creation," the one who for all eternity God has thought to call into a relationship with himself, and with whom God can share his very self.

If then, as John the apostle says, God is "life" (1 Jn 5:20) and "God is light" (1 Jn 1:5), this means that the mystery of God is a mystery of life that is love and specifies that it is a love that is all-spiritual, all-light. Spicq comments, "Like a sun that illuminates and shines, like a spring of water that comes forth and gives life, God is pure charity, who loves by expressing and giving himself. This communication and sharing of himself is his nature, and thus it is his law of life."[2]

Furthermore, "God is Spirit" (Jn 4:24), as Jesus affirms when speaking with the Samaritan woman. This refers to more than that God has immateriality: he is the always new and integral force of life and of communion. This is the strongest confirmation that God's essence is love, a gift of himself—a gift of himself to the humanity and therefore, a gift of himself, a communion of himself within his very own self between the Father and the Son who are one in the Spirit.

Indeed God is love for us because he is love in himself. God establishes a communion between him and us because in his very nature from all eternity he is a communion of love in himself.[3]

"The Father (the origin, without beginning, of love) insofar as he only gives of himself," Kasper explains, "cannot exist without the Son who receives this gift. The Son . . . exists in as much as he receives everything from the Father and returns everything back to the Father. . . . However, this reciprocal love wishes to transcend itself. It is a pure gift only if it strips and frees itself from the duality, and through pure grace introduces a third, in whom love is only a receiving, and exists only in as much as it receives from the common love that the Father and Son hold for one another."[4]

It is the mystery of the one and triune God. From all eternity, in his unique essence—which is love—he exists trinitarianly, that is, differentiating (because he is love and a total gift of himself) into the persons of the Father, the Son and the Spirit, therefore in an "ineffable 'plural,'"[5] which at the same time is perfect unity.

"In truth," Augustine writes, "you see the Trinity if you see love." "They are three: the lover, the loved, and love." "And not more than three: one who loves the one who comes from him, one who loves the one from whom he came, and love itself. . . . And if this doesn't mean anything, in what way can it be that *God is love*? And if there is no substance here, in what way is God substance?"[6]

By introducing us into a communion of love with him already here on this earth—through grace, which is the gift of his very life—God makes us capable of establishing a similar relationship of love among ourselves. "*As the Father* has loved me," Jesus said, "*so* I have loved you" (Jn 15:9). He loved us, therefore, with the same love with which he and the Father love one another. But he has also told us to love one another with the same love: "*such as my* love has been for you, *so must your* love be for each other" (Jn 13:34; cf. 15:12-17).[7] This has become possible through the gift of the Spirit that has been given to us.

"There is an affinity then," Chiara comments, "between the Father, the Son and us . . . through the one divine love that we possess."[8]

One divine agape unites in the Spirit: the Father and the Son, the Son and the sons and daughters, and the sons and daughters—in the Son—with the Father and among themselves.

For this reason Jesus can ask the Father, according to his design, that the disciples may reach the fullness of unity that there is between him and the Father. "That all may be one *as* you, Father, are in me, and I in you; I pray that they may be [one] in us" (Jn 17:21).

This, Latourelle writes, is "the design of the Father": "the extension of the same trinitarian life to all of humanity. Through Christ, the Father wants to associate us to the relationships of sonship and spiration of the trinitarian life. He wants to re-generate his own Son in every human being. He wants to infuse his Spirit into them and unite everyone to one another in the most intimate communion, so that all may be one, as the Father and the Son are one in the same Spirit of love."[9]

The response of love by Chiara and her companions to God-Love, which is, as we have seen, the unconditional adherence to his will, was concentrated, already in the early months of their new life, in a radical commitment to live reciprocal love. In the commandment of Jesus, they took literally that *"as* I have loved you," that is, the disposition, which they outwardly declared, to give their lives for one another as Jesus did.

Their faithfulness to reciprocal love and to the divine model, Jesus crucified and forsaken, soon opened up for them an ever more vibrant life of unity. "Do you know to what point we must love one another?" Chiara, under the impulse of the Holy Spirit, said one day to those around her: "To the point of consuming ourselves into one."[10]

Jesus' prayer for unity (cf. Jn 17) became their "magna carta."[11] A light shone on these words and they were translated into life, into all the events of daily life, by all those who came into contact with and adhered to the Focolare.

This supernatural unity has as its source, model and end the Trinity, to which they spontaneously looked in order to understand and to explain to the others how to proceed in the life they had undertaken.

However, in its turn, the experience they were living opened their hearts and minds to continually new aspects of this first and fundamental mystery, while always remaining a mystery, of the unity and trinity of God.

As we have already mentioned, an authentic experience is also a source for the theological deepening of Christian truths. In our age, Muhlen observes, "access to the mystery of the Most Holy Trinity is no longer a purely speculative effort, but a concrete attempt to be fully conformed, in faith, to the mysterious reality that takes place among us and in us." He adds that obviously "what happens among us and in us is more than what we are conscientiously aware of."[12]

The Tri-unity of God who is love

In the experience and thought of Chiara we find clear

evidence from the very beginning of the essential elements of a *rich teaching on the unity and the trinity of God.* Chiara speaks about this within the sphere of an *equally rich teaching on unity among the lives of human beings* and of an intense life of unity lived among her and her companions, founded on Christ and shaped by the trinitarian life.

In a letter of 1948 Chiara writes, "The Ideal we have embraced is *God-Unity-Trinity*, and therefore, it is as ineffable as infinite and eternal love."

After highlighting that if two are united in the name of Christ—that is if they love one another as he loved us—he is in their midst (cf. Mt 18:20) and in each of them (cf. Gal 2:20), she goes on to say:

> The important thing is to make *unity* the foundation, means and the end.
>
> In this unity desired by God the two souls are fused into *one* and reappear *equal and distinct.* As in the Most Holy Trinity.
>
> Jesus wanted it in his testament, which is the synthesis of all his thoughts! The thoughts of a God!
>
> "May they all be one, as you and I . . ."[13]

In a page written in 1946, wherein she explains the dynamics of unity among human beings and its relationship with the trinitarian life, Chiara explains that the basis of the unity and the trinity of God is love.

"Only Christ," Chiara says, "can make two into *one*, because his love, which is the emptiness of self (love infused in us by the Holy Spirit), allows us to reach the depths of other peoples' hearts." Then the Trinity comes to live within individuals and among them (cf. Jn 14:23) because in the one "who empties oneself" and "among the two" who are united by emptying themselves one in the other, out of love, "Christ relives, and in Christ, the

Father." Among the two who live in this way a trinitarian relationship comes to life: "I in you and you in me." Chiara goes on to say that this kind of unity demands love for others which is the "emptying of self," so that Christ can live in each. From this unity everyone reappears as equal and distinct. The reason and the basis for these dynamics lies in the fact that unity among human persons is a sharing in the life of the one and triune God. In the same text she says:

> God is *one and triune*. Because of their very same nature, which is love, the three live in unifying themselves (by emptying themselves) and in doing so they each re-find themselves.... The three make themselves one out of love, and in the One Love, they rediscover themselves.[14]

The life of unity, wherein Jesus is present in the midst of those who love one another as he loved, is the topic also of the following text through which Chiara speaks even further on the trinitarian mystery.

> When he (Jesus) is among us we are *one* and we are *three*, each equal to the *one*....
> What happens between you and me is what happens among the persons of the Trinity....
> The Holy Spirit is third after the Father and the Son. He proceeds from both. But he is still *ab aeterno* with the two.
> In fact, how can we suppose that there is a Father who generates and loves the Son if Love is not in him? And how can we suppose there is a Son who loves if Love is not in him? Yet, he (Love) proceeds from the other two and is third (so to speak).[15]

The text goes on by illustrating that where there is reciprocal love, where there is unity, because Jesus is among his people and they in him are in the Father, the trinitarian life "flows freely" in them. Thus they come to experience it more fully. This life is already in them through grace, but by living in this way they can share it with their brothers and sisters, so that they too might rediscover in themselves the divine life they already possess.

The intra-trinitarian dynamism of God-Love

Chiara develops further the analogy between the life of unity and distinction among human persons and the life of the Trinity.

> We will be a reflection of the Trinity wherein the Father is distinct from the Son and from the Spirit, though still containing in himself the Son and the Holy Spirit: the Father, therefore, equal to the Spirit, who contains in himself the Father and the Son, and equal to the Son, who contains in himself the Father and the Holy Spirit.[16]

This particular reflection on the Trinity forms the basis for one of the more frequently used explanations that Chiara gives of the life of unity among the members of the Focolare. The unity she speaks of is always understood as unity and distinction, in the sense that, the more they consume themselves in one, the more equal they become, that is, each one becomes another Christ. At the same time each becomes more distinct because each individual personality is enhanced by this life of unity.

Here Chiara calls to mind a particular effect, which is also a witness, of such a life of unity, describing it as, "a reflection" on earth of the trinitarian life.

In order to explain what happens in the unity among them Chiara uses an analogy, which is obviously imperfect like every analogy between created things and the Creator. She compares their unity with what happens in the Uni-trinity of God, where the persons are distinct from one another, even though each of the three "contains" the other two, and they are equal, precisely because in each one there are the other two.

The Fathers and Doctors of the Church speak of the *perichoresis* of the three divine persons. That is to say that in their reciprocal giving and acceptance, they are dynamically one in the other, so that in each one of the three the other two are present.

The perfect perichoresis of the persons of the Trinity, founded on the unity of their nature which is love and which implies the unity of their reciprocal love, synthesizes all that has been revealed on the Three who are One.[17]

The New Testament reveals the mutual indwelling of the three divine persons and affirms their being "one:" "I am in the Father and the Father is in me" (Jn 14:11); "The Father and I are one" (Jn 10:30).[18] The tradition of the Church, since its very beginning, gives to this a doctrinal explanation.[19]

John Damascene expresses the dynamic interpenetration of the persons of the Trinity in this way: "The remaining and residing of one in the other of the three Persons means that they ... have a reciprocal perichoresis that is without confusion, not in the way of a blending or mixing together, but in the way of joining themselves to one another. ... This movement is one and identical, because there is only one impetus and dynamism of the three persons."[20]

Fulgentius of Ruspe, who reflects the Latin position, which is inclined more than Greek thought to explain perichoresis as being an interconnection of the persons based on the one divine substance, writes: "The Father is all in the Son and all in the Holy Spirit; the Son is all in the Father and all in the Holy Spirit; the Holy Spirit is all in the Father and all in the Son."[21] This is the phrasing that would be later adopted by the Council of Florence (1442) to describe the doctrine of the circumincession[22] between the divine persons.[23]

In any case, the trinitarian mystery remains unfathomable, impossible to express through one image alone or with one concept alone. Gregory of Nazianzen writes in an exemplary way: "As soon as I start to ponder Unity, I am overwhelmed by the splendor of the Trinity. And as soon as I start to ponder the Trinity, I am completely taken by Unity."[24]

The One who is the Three and the Three who are One is the more appropriate dimension of God. Since it is God's dimension, it is also that of the entire reality he created; it is its most mysterious dimension.

All the same, we can still have an intuition of this mystery if we reflect on what happens, though mysteriously, in believers who through a free gift of God have been given a participation in this reality.

They certainly cannot penetrate one another as do the divine persons, but God can penetrate them and make them one.

De Margerie writes, "Christ invites us to believe in the relationships of reciprocal in-existence (meaning 'existing in') between the Father and him, so that we might later come to know them in the beatific vision, or at least, in their mystical anticipation (cf. Jn 14:11-20), that is, through the practice of the mutual in-existence of unifying charity among Christians as well as among them, on one side, and the Father and the Son, on the other (cf. Jn 17:21: 'may they be one in us').

"The practice of the imperfect created mutual in-existence and of the intersubjectivity of love constitutes therefore, for the New Testament, the condition for the full unveiling, in the beatific vision, of the perfect uncreated mutual in-existence and intersubjectivity of the Father and of the Son in the Holy Spirit."[25]

It is possible, therefore, to have a perichoresis among believers, even though it is imperfect, through the vertical perichoresis, so to speak, that exists between them and the Trinity by way of Christ in the Holy Spirit: "I living in them, you living in me" (Jn 17:23), "I am in the Father, and you in me, and I in you" (Jn 14:20).

Unity among human persons "as" among the divine persons, can occur only in God: "That they may be [one] *in us*" (Jn 17:21). Only God can produce it. It is his gift. That is why Jesus asks the Father for it and why he tells the disciples to love one another as the persons in the Trinity love one another: "As the Father loves me, so also I love you"; "As I have loved you, so you also should love one another."

He showed the utmost expression and measure of such a love—toward the Father and toward humanity—on the cross. There he "emptied himself" (Phil 2:7) to the point of experiencing the abandonment of the Father, which he expressed in his cry, "My God, my God, why have you forsaken me?" (Mk 15:34). This act is the translation into the human condition of the love of the Word in the Trinity:[26] an infinite emptiness of self, a total gift of self as Word to the Father as an absolute nothingness, which is *love* however, and therefore *is*, and is eternally the Son. He is the answer to the total gift of self—the infinite emptiness—that is the Father, who is the first to give all of himself. It could be said that the Father empties himself, that he makes himself nothing, since to give everything here on earth includes "losing," becoming "empty"—instead, *he is*, because *he is love*. It is the Father who eternally generates the Son. And from their unconditional mutual love proceeds the Holy Spirit, love made person.

"Three . . ." Chiara writes, "form the Trinity, yet they are one, because love *is and is not* at the same time. But also when it *is not*, it *is*, because it is love." She continues the explanation with an example: "If I renounce something and *give* it away (I deprive myself of it—*it is not*) out of love, *I have love*—therefore it *is*."[27]

It is the paradox of love, that it *is not*, meaning it does not exist for itself, and for that reason it *is*, for it is love.[28] It is the dynamism of trinitarian love, through which the divine persons are eternally One while still remaining Three.

A similar reality—Chiara can say through an enlightenment and an experience sparked within her by the Spirit—is imprinted by God in the relationships among human persons. "I felt that I have been created as a gift for the person next to me and the person next to me has been created by God as a gift for me. Just as the Father in the Trinity is everything for the Son and the Son is everything for the Father."[29] And, "the relationship among us is the Holy Spirit, which is the same relationship that exists among the persons of the Trinity."[30]

It is the Father who, through the Son incarnate, has communicated to human beings the one who is the very relationship among them. He wants to make them capable of living "as the Trinity" already here on earth to the point of the full realization in heaven. The Holy Spirit, in turn, animates and strengthens love among human beings, and makes them one. He introduces them into the Trinity, into the heart of the relationships among the divine persons, who enwrap and penetrate them, thus transfiguring their beings and their reciprocal relationships into the image of the Trinity.

In the writings of Chiara just previously cited, we find clearly recognizable hints of a new foundation for the whole discussion of being and this comes out of a new penetration of trinitarian ontology. In such a discussion, a conception of reality can be viewed through the primary place given, not to substance, but to the person, which is considered essentially in the relationship of giving and receiving. It is a conception, therefore, that is molded on intra-trinitarian love, and reveals in love the fundamental basis and deepest meaning of being. This is the idea that arises from Chiara's experience. By incorporating herself into the dynamism of the same divine self-giving—"into the movement of love which is God himself"[31]—Chiara, in her turn, gives herself completely, in the totality of her being and in her relationship with others. This entire reality, then, reveals itself to Chiara with that trinitarian mark which constitutes her own being and inner life, opening up for her new avenues toward an ever more profound understanding of the trinitarian mystery.

The Trinity living in the individual

From what we have seen so far, it appears evident that the new commandment lived with Christ's measure of love is "a little reflection of the trinitarian life" on earth.[32] If two or more live it, *not only does the Trinity* live *in each of them*—"Anyone who loves me will be true to my word, and my Father will love him; we will come to him" (Jn 14:23)—*but also in their unity* there is "a single

Trinity where the two are as Father and Son and among them is the Holy Spirit."[33]

Both of these dimensions which the trinitarian mystery can shape in believers are found in the members of the Focolare, as we can read in numerous writings of Chiara.

The contents of the following texts are profound and luminous in their treatment of the *Trinity living in the individual*.

> The Trinity within me!
> The abyss within me!
> Immensity within me!
> The boundless depths of love within me!
> The Father whom Jesus proclaimed to us within me!
> The Word!
> The Holy Spirit, whom I want to have always
>   in order to serve the Focolare, within me!
> I do not ask for more.
> I want to live in this abyss, to lose myself in this sun,
>   to dwell together with Life Eternal.[34]

I too have felt for some time the attraction to "live within" where, if I am in grace, there is the Most Holy Trinity.

> The Father enwraps me
> in his loving heart,
> the Word kisses me
> that impelling ray,
> the Holy Spirit
> a gentle breeze
> the soul embraces
> so white a dove.
> The Trinity reigns inside of me.[35]

The trinitarian indwelling is the real and true presence of all three of the divine persons who give themselves, in the totality and in the personal uniqueness of their being love, to those who love, in order to draw them always further into their communion.[36] This reality reaches lofty expression in these texts of Chiara. We find in these words a living witness to the perichoresis between Creator and creature which, in the reciprocal giving of love, unites God with the human person and the human person with God in the same breath of life and of knowledge. St. Bernard felt this to such a degree that he exclaimed: "O happy union, if you have experienced it. . . . Yes, you do well if you adhere to God with all your being. But who adheres so perfectly to God? Those who, loved by God, dwell in him, and by loving him in their turn, attract him to themselves. Therefore, when the human person and God are united to one another in every way, since the profound and mutual love makes them enter into the hearts of one another, God is in that person and that person is in God."[37]

The Trinity present among those who are united in the name of Christ

We have already examined in some of Chiara's writings the reality of the *Trinity present among two or more persons united in the name of Christ*.

However, there is one particular page which, in its clarity and simplicity, illustrates a fundamental experience that opened a new phase of life for the Focolare. It refers to a period "of special graces," a period of light, which—in the summer of 1949—outlined God's plan for the newborn Focolare movement.

Unimagined circumstances, but foreseen by providence, brought the initial group of the Focolare to go to rest . . . in the mountains. . . .

> We were alone, just among ourselves, together with our great Ideal which we were living moment by moment, together with Jesus in the eucharist, the bond of unity, whom we were drawn to each day. We were alone in our rest, prayer, and meditation.
> And so began a period of special graces.
> We had the impression that the Lord opened the eyes of our souls to the kingdom of God which was among us: the Trinity which lives in a cell of the Mystical Body: "O Father most holy, protect them with your name which you have given me [that they may be one, even as we are one]" (Jn 17:11).[38]

The eyes of faith are opened to the Trinity present among those who, because they are united in the name of Christ, form a living cell of the Mystical Body. In other words, the indwelling of the Uni-trinity of God unveils itself in its collective dimension—typical of the spirituality of the Focolare—which always presupposes and at the same time enhances the personal dimension.

It is an extraordinary experience of the trinitarian life which is heaven "already" present in each of us and among us. It is the beginning of what is to come in the fullness of escatological times. For this reason Chiara, continuing her writing, says:

> Naturally we would never have come down from that mountain, that little Tabor of our soul, if God's will had not shown us differently. It was only our love for Jesus crucified and forsaken, who lives in a humanity immersed in darkness, that gave us the courage to do it.[39]

Having returned then, only out of love for him, into the midst of the world where life runs on oblivious of the divine, and having made herself competely one with the Trinity inside of her while looking upon those around her with the eyes of God, Chiara discovered the same reality within them, and enkindled it. Consequently, many living cells of the Mystical Body were coming to life and in each cell and among all of them there dwelled the Trinity.

Chiara writes in a most profound way:

> I would call my Ideal a utopia if I didn't think of him, who also saw a world like this around him, and who at the height of his life seemed overwhelmed by it, as though evil had defeated him.
>
> He too looked out upon this great crowd which he loved as he loved himself. He who was God, who had created everyone, would have wanted to extend the bonds that were to unite all to himself, as children to their Father, and to unite brothers and sisters to one another.
>
> He had come to bring the family back together, to make all people one. . . .
>
> He looked at the world just as I see it, but he didn't doubt. . . .
>
> He looked at the world as he prayed at night to heaven above and to heaven within him, where the Trinity dwelled and was the true Being, the Everything that was real, while outside on the streets there wandered about the nothingness that passes away.
>
> And I am doing the same as he did in order to remain bound to the eternal, to the uncreated, which is the root of the created, and therefore, the life of everything. . . .
>
> I look at the world that is within of me and I hold on to what has being and value. I make myself

completely one with the Trinity who rests in my soul and who enlightens it with eternal light, filling it with the whole of heaven, inhabited by the angels and saints who . . . can all be found in my little being recollected with the Three in a unity of love.

And I encounter the fire, which invades the whole humanity God gave me and makes me another Christ, another God-man by participation. My humanity merges with the divine. My eyes are no longer closed. I look at the world and everything in it with the pupil of my eye, a void to my soul, through which all the light that is within me passes (if I allow God to live in me). But it is no longer I who look, it is Christ in me who looks and sees once again the blind to be enlightened, the dumb to be given voice, and the crippled to be healed. Blind to the vision of God within and outside of themselves. Deaf to the word of God who speaks also in them and who through them could be transmitted to others and thus awaken the truth in them. Crippled because they have become immobilized, and are ignorant of the divine will which in the depths of their hearts spurs them on to the eternal movement that is eternal love, where by spreading the fire one becomes inflamed.

In this way, opening my eyes to what is outside of me, I see humanity with the eyes of God, who is all-trusting, because he is Love.

I see and discover in the others my own light, my true reality, my true self . . . and having found myself again, I unite myself to myself [in them], reviving myself—as love which is life—in my neighbor.

In this way I revive Jesus, another Christ, another God-man, the manifestation of the Father's goodness here on earth, the eyes of God on humanity. Thus I extend Christ in me in my neighbor and I form a living and complete cell of the Mystical Body of Christ, a living cell, a hearth of God, which possesses the fire that is to be communicated, along with its light, to others.

It is God who from two makes one, placing himself as third, as the relation between them: Jesus among us.

In this way love circulates and (through its inherent law of communion) naturally carries along with it, like a river of fire, all that the two possess, in order to put both their material and spiritual goods into common.

This gives a living and visible witness of unifying love, of true love, the love of the Trinity.

Truly, therefore, the total Christ relives in both of us, in each of us, and among us.

And I think that by allowing God to live in me, and by allowing him to love himself in my neighbors, he will discover himself in many, and their eyes will beam with his light.[40]

The trinitarian life, "I in you and you in me," reveals its essence: the deepest reality that pervades the whole life "of the Mystical Body, modeled on the Most Holy Trinity,"[41] both in its entirety and in each of its cells.

The above text, though only partially quoted, attests, like many other writings especially of that period, to the novelty and the completeness of a trinitarian doctrine that is ahead of its time and is still today quite original. The rich content, the fervid language, together as always with the testimony of life, shed light on and render accessible the depths of the trinitarian mystery and its fruitful dynamism, both within its own being and in its operations in history.

The entire life of the Focolare has been steadily built on the model of the Trinity: its spirituality, its structure, the relationships among its members and among the various branches, its activities and dialogues with other Christians, with the faithful of other religions, and with non-believers.[42]

Already in 1948 Chiara noted that "the mark of the Unity and Trinity of God is present throughout the whole Focolare movement."[43]

In the years that followed, the Second Vatican Council brought the trinitarian vision of the Church and of the world back into focus. The Council presented the Church as the Church of the Trinity, the icon of the one and triune God, defining it, in the words of Cyprian, as "a people brought into unity from the unity of the Father and of the Son and of the Holy Spirit."[44] "She is filled with the Trinity," affirms Origen,[45] and she is its mysterious extension in the midst of humanity and in the evolution of the world, for humanity and for the world.[46]

All men and women, therefore, are "called to share in the intimate life of God, in whose image they are created. They are called to live in reciprocal communion among themselves, in love, modelled on God who is love, which is unity in the Trinity. They are called to be a reflection in the world of the communion of love that lies in him."[47] The new community of humanity will thus receive its life and form from "its trinitarian roots."[48] The human family will become the dwelling place of God—filled in itself with the Trinity.

Chapter 5

TRINITARIAN LOVE IN THE WORKINGS OF THE THREE DIVINE PERSONS

As we have seen, God, trinitarian Love, has made himself known to Chiara in his deepest essence and allows himself to be experienced in his dwelling as the Trinity of love in the midst of humanity as well as in each individual.

In a further development Chiara penetrates the immanent mystery of God the Trinity: in his expressing himself "outside" of himself, which is a fruitful communion of being and of life; in his free and gratuitous sharing of himself, through the supreme gift of Christ, to a humanity in need of salvation; in his conducting the course of history toward its fulfillment, which lies in the total revelation and gift of himself.

She speaks about the trinitarian giving of self on the part of God-Love for us in several profound writings: "He is . . . love. He is the creator, our redeemer, the sanctifier."[1] "We believe in God who is love, who created us out of love, who redeemed us out of love, who desires our salvation out of love, and who requires our love . . . so that he can give himself—Love—to us."[2]

Therefore, in the unfolding of the divine economy, trinitarian love reveals and communicates itself according to the specific workings of the Father, of the Son and of the Holy Spirit in the life of creation, in the history of humanity, and in each person.

The Creator

A number of Chiara's writings, dating back principally to a period of intense enlightenment, reveal her penetrating discovery of the uni-trinitarian dimension imprinted by God in the being he created. She underlines the "trinitarian mark of the Creator" which is present in the entire universe in the vital interrelationships of the basic elements that constitute it: "matter; the law that governs it, almost like the gospel of nature; and life, a consequence of the unity of the first two. These elements as a whole, in continuing to 'live,' present the image of the unity of God, the God of the living."[3]

All of creation, therefore, in being a reflection of the unity-distinction proper to the one and triune God, manifests itself in its true reality: the mysterious expansion of the free self-giving of trinitarian Love "outside" of himself and the extension, in time, of his eternal dynamism. Shaped on the model of the intimate communication of God in God, wherein the Father generates the Son and the Holy Spirit emanates from their mutual love, creation becomes a reflection of the same uncreated mystery.

The magisterium and tradition of the Church have constantly affirmed that the Trinity is "the sole principle of the universe,"[4] in virtue of the one being, the one life, and the one love that are common to all three of the divine persons. Augustine affirms, "If the Father, the Son and the Holy Spirit are one single God, one single world has been made by the Father, through the Son, in the Spirit."[5] The Son and the Spirit are therefore co-creators with the Father: the three are one creator. "The Father," von Balthasar explains, "created the world in the Son and to the Son's glory; the Son also created it and saved it to the Father's glory in order to present it, having been made perfect, to the Father (cf. 1 Cor 15:24-28). Finally the Spirit enlightens it not to reveal himself, but to reveal the infinite love between the Father and the Son and to incorporate this love in creation."[6]

Therefore, the always new understanding of the transcendence and the infinite love of God the creator, which comes from contemplating the immensity of the universe and its extraordinary beauty and power, becomes a praise to him, a praise to the Trinity. In sharing her personal experience, Chiara relates: "I understood, as never before, who is the one we had chosen as our Ideal, or better, who is the one who had chosen us. I saw him so great, so great, so great, that it seemed impossible to me that he would have thought of us. . . . Now when I pray 'Hallowed be your name' or 'Glory be to the Father, to the Son, and to the Holy Spirit' it is something entirely different for me. It has become a need of the heart."[7]

Out of this trinitarian theophany, which the universe shows itself to be, there emerges an even more profound knowlege of Being, made visible through the universe. It is what Chiara highlights when she recognizes that love is the essence of all things: of the uncreated, of the created, and of the very relationship between the uncreated and the created.

God is the one who is and God is love. And . . . everything is love: love uncreated and love created. However, even love created is joined to the Creator by a bond of unity, which love itself created, and which makes the Creator a single entity with the created: a single entity of love.

God is Being and this Being is love. It is a Being that gives life to other beings, who are like expansions of this love. In any case they are love and have life because they are rooted in God and are one with God, though distinct (from him), because they are created. . . .

Here lies the mystery of life that God gives to all things.[8]

God-Love sustains all things by his continuous creative act. He orders and moves them in a wondrous unity that preserves distinction, not only between the uncreated and the created, but among all things themselves. Chiara writes:

> If we could see beyond the veil of creation, we would find the one who sustains all that we see, the one who orders and moves all things. And we would see such a cohesion, such closeness, such unity, though keeping distinction, of the created with the uncreated to leave us in awe.
>
> It is not so rare that mystics have had intuitions or intellectual visions reflecting this. . . .
>
> In a way stronger than what the eye can see as distinct and separated, for instance, a flower, the sky, a stream, the sun, the moon, the sea, the night, or the day, these mystics have seen a loving Light that supports and joins everything together, as though creation were a single song of love. It is as though the rocks and the snow, the fields and the stars were in their deepest essence so fused in that Light and among themselves that as a consequence they were created as a gift for one another, as though each were in love with the other.
>
> This must have been the experience, one can imagine, of the loved-filled mind of St. Francis and thus the deepest inspiration of the "Canticle of the Creatures" that poured forth from his heart.
>
> When he calls the sun brother and the water sister, he is not being poetic or sentimental, but affirms a truth of which he intuited. . . . He captures the unity that exists throughout the whole universe.

And, having discovered the Creator of all things, who is the father of each one, he sees them all, though in different ways, related to one another.[9]

Spidlik observes, "Such a vision of God in the created reality is . . . given only to those who are pure of heart, and trained in the practice of the commandments, above all in charity, which makes them similar to God. It is an intuitive knowledge. . . . This experience consists in the mysterious sharing in the knowledge possessed by the Word, the Son of God, in the heart of the trinitarian life."[10]

Furthermore, those who love live in God who is love and "see," says Chiara, that "in this world everyone is at the center, because the law of everything is love." They discover the divine plan which God "designed for us and for our brothers and sisters, where everything falls into a splendid scheme of love," where "a mysterious bond of love links persons and things, guides history, orders the destiny of peoples and individuals, while respecting their freedom to the full."[11]

Every event then, be it great or insignificant, acquires new meaning and opens the mind to the wider visions of life, to the profound sense of history. In the unfolding affairs of daily life, Chiara observes, one can discover a golden thread, "which seems to tie everything together, to reorder, even harmonize or in any case lead all things toward a good and greater end." The realization comes that throughout the world today it is necessary, even "indispensable, to call attention back to the true Christian vision of life."[12]

The Redeemer

But the greatest manifestation of God's love for the world is the gift of his Son who became man for all of humanity (cf. Jn 3:16).

"In him," Chiara writes, "love took on its form par excellence."[13]

"We could perhaps imagine God as a Father . . . but God as a brother, who in heaven adores with us his and our Father, is such a mystery that it can only be grasped if we recognize that God is truly love."[14] Love who became flesh, who lives as a man in the midst of humanity, and who dies on the cross in order to reunite all people to the Father, makes them sharers of his divine sonship through the gift of the Spirit, and thus makes them in every way similar to himself.

Reading the entire historical and salvific event of Christ with the light of love, Chiara concludes: "The Son of God who is love, came to this earth out of love, he lived out of love . . . giving love, bringing the law of love, and dying out of love. He then resurrected and ascended to heaven, thus completing his design of love."[15] Having come upon earth, therefore, he brought "the very love that burns ardently in God," "the way of life of the Trinity," so that "we may live as those in heaven live, that we may live the way God lives."[16]

God showed his love for us most sublimely, however, by living, in a mysterious but real way, the experience of suffering,[17] by suffering together with us and for us.

God's com-passionate love reached its culmination on the cross. The moment had come to bridge the distance— the infinite distance caused by sin—that separated us from the Father and to unite us to him. In that moment Jesus, the Son of God, he himself who was God, Love, reached the point of experiencing, out of love—in the infinite distance of himself from the Father, of God from God—the abandonment of God, where we ourselves were found. He experienced the abandonment to the point of making himself nothing.[18] The measure of this complete abandonment was the handing over to the Father of the eternal bond of unity which bound Jesus to the Father: the Holy Spirit.[19] In this total abandonment, in his making himself nothing, which is his most sublime act of love, he became all Love, the Love, also in his humanity. He became the source, therefore, of the Spirit of love which reunites all of us to the Father and among ourselves.[20]

In this trinitarian perspective, the paschal event of Christ reveals itself in its reality of love, of that love that God is for us for the very reason that he is love in himself. The "condition that opens the possibility" to this salvific event "lies in the intimate life of the trinitarian God." This is so because "the relationship of the Father with the incarnate Son in the consummation of the gift of the Spirit is the same constitutional relationship of the Trinity,"[21] it is absolute love. Von Balthasar explains: "The act with which the Father expresses and gives away his entire divinity (an act that he not only 'does,' but 'is'), in generating the Son as one infinitely other than himself, can only be, at the same time, the eternal condition that overcomes all division and alienation in the world and is in the same act, a gift of love, of the possiblity of relationship, of happiness. . . . That God (as Father) can in this manner give away his divinity, and that God (as Son) does not receive it as though only on loan, but possesses it in an 'equality of essence,' signifies such an inconceivable and insurmountable 'separation' of God from himself that any other kind of separation that may occur as such . . . be it most bitter and dark, can find its explanation only inside of this one. This is true even though this same communication is an event of absolute love,"[22] an event that occurs in the Holy Spirit, who is the personal *expression* of the greatest distinction of the Father from the Son and, at the same time, of their most perfect unity.

In the mystery of the unfathomable abandonment of Jesus, which Chiara so deeply penetrated, "we contemplated . . . immediately," she writes, "the *summit of his love because it was the summit of his pain.* In fact, Jesus forsaken reveals *all* the love of a God." And so "what was perceived in him and his immense pain was the unfurling of his love." This "inspired us to value our own pain, as an expression of our love for him," and by uniting our suffering to his—as God came down to earth: redeemer of the world—"to become co-redeemers in him and with him."[23]

The choice of God for Chiara and her companions became more precisely defined as the choice of Jesus forsaken: "The God of love we chose lives in him."[24]

Chiara continues by recalling the time of that fundamental enlightenment and its consequent choice of life. In loving him forsaken in every suffering, they found love, they found God. Beyond suffering that is loved, she writes, "we truly understood what love is, we became fused with Love and we shared in its light." "We felt like we were contemplating the immense love that God poured out over the world." We saw that "it is from the pain of the Crucified, reaching its climax in that cry, that redemption, sanctification and deification come."[25]

From here arose, as Chiara expressed in a letter of the early times, "the infinite desire to love Love more than all the hearts of the world" and the impulse to generate that same love "in thousands of hearts." "What a multitude of saints!" she then foresees. "What heaven on earth through Love forsaken!"[26]

Even more, love for Jesus forsaken is the way, the secret wherein we not only find God, Love, but we unite ourselves to him. We become him by participation, as Chiara writes in a well-known page of 1949: "Jesus forsaken, embraced... chosen as our one and only all... consumed in one with us, while we are consumed in one with him, turned into suffering with him who is Suffering. This is everything. This is how we become... God, Love."[27]

Jesus, the incarnate Son of God ("consumed in one with us"), gave ("consumed") everything of himself to the Father and to us. He "made himself nothing" out of love and became—also in his humanity—all love. Consequently, when we exclusively desire him ("consumed in one with him"), by making ourselves nothing, he can hand over and share with us his own life, the divine life, which is Love, and allow us to become God, Love.[28]

The Sanctifier

The divine dynamism of love, as we have noted, is this: it gives everything (it has not), it gives itself (it is not), therefore it is. It is life that is always new and overflowing with joy, light, love, unity and freedom. This is what happens in the heart of the intra-trinitarian relationships, and in the workings of love of the Trinity through which God communicates himself in creation and in the divine redemption of humanity.

The reality of the Holy Spirit is the free, superabundant giving of love in the reciprocal gift of self between the Father and the Son. He is their bond of Love, "Love become person in the heart of the Trinity which is all love."[29]

The Spirit expresses, therefore, God's deepest essence: love in the intimate communion among the divine persons, therefore in the deepest inwardness of the one and triune God, which at the same time is the greatest interdivine outwardness. The intra-trinitarian reality of God's "being outside of himself" is accomplished in the Spirit of love. In the Spirit of love lies the presupposition and the fulfillment of God's self-giving *ad extra,* of the communication of himself through grace, in a continuous creative act that renews the world of the original creation. Thus the world is reshaped according to God's very being: according to the agape of the one and triune God.

It is in this love, in the Holy Spirit, that God gives being to all that exists. In this love he recomposes the unity of all human beings with him and among themselves. This is the love he gives us so that we might become similar to him, saints; that is, perfect in love, perfect in unity, because God, the saint, is love,[30] he is unity in the Trinity. Guided by him, we carry ahead in history and in the world the unfolding of his plan of love.

To this person of the Trinity, to Love hypostatisized, Chiara entrusts our sanctity: "Oh! Holy Spirit, Spirit of love, in whom Love—which is God—is made a person. You . . . Spirit who mold saints—perhaps more than anyone you desire and love to assist us in this one task which is worth giving our lives for. . . ."[31] He is the sanctifier.

It is the Holy Spirit—the mutual gift between the Father and the Son—who accomplishes the divinization of men and women. He makes them capable of responding, with the gift of their own selves, to the gift that the Father, through Christ and in the Spirit, makes of himself to them. In this way they become similar to his Son and the divine glory of the Trinity shines in them, as it does in him.[32]

It is the Holy Spirit—the bond of love, the unity be-another, we send off, from the total death of ourselves, a single flame: the Holy Spirit, the Spirit of the Risen Lord in our midst."[35]

This is the height of our sharing in the trinitarian life of love: to "breathe," in the Father and in the Son, the Holy Spirit, their Spirit of love.[36]

In this way, also through us, he can advance his work, which is the deification of every human person, of the Church and of humanity. It is a work that was begun by the crucified and risen Lord, and will be brought to completion by the Holy Spirit. And the entire universe, through humanity that is divinized, will also be always more and more transfigured into "new heavens" and "new earth" (cf. Rv 21:1), "deified," made, that is, a sharer in the same "glory of the sons of God" (cf. Rom 8:21).

Through the Holy Spirit, by way of the mediation of the glorified Son, the movement to return all creation to the Father will be accomplished: "everything began from love and through love returns to love."[37]

tween the Father and the Son—who works and who is the same unity between humankind and God. "By means of the one who is the love of the Father and of the Son," William Saint Thierry writes, "the unity, the gentleness, the good, the kiss, the embrace and all that is common to them . . . the very relationship that joins in substantial unity the Son to the Father and the Father to the Son becomes also established, in certain fashion, between humankind and God. In some way, the same loving awareness is found at the center of the embrace and the kiss of the Father and of the Son. So then, in an ineffable and inconceivable way, a person of God merits to become, not God, but what God is, since the human person becomes, through the effects of grace, what God is in virtue of his own nature."[33]

It is through the Holy Spirit that the believers are "one" among themselves. It is through him that they form a family of the children of God, destined—as Chiara points out—to extend itself to all humankind in virtue of its own life. "In fact, it is he," she writes, "who binds in unity the members of the Mystical Body. It is he whom Jesus sent down upon the apostles and then upon us for the fulfillment of his prayer of unity. It was the Holy Spirit who gave us the charism that we possess (a charism of unity). . . . He is the one who will bring about the unity of Christians. He is the one who will enlighten those distant from God. He is God-Love."[34]

We must, therefore, make room for him by living among ourselves, docile to his impulses, the same dynamics of the intra-trinitarian life.

In recalling a text of a Father of the Church, Chiara says, "Just as the Father and the Son, in loving one another, produce (like two burning logs crossed over one another) a single flame: the Holy Spirit," so too, in loving one another as they do, "in burning like many logs crossed over one

MARY—THE RADIANT IMAGE OF GOD WHO IS LOVE

God's design of love for humanity has already been fulfilled in one of its members, the first to be fully deified: Mary.

In Mary the trinitarian mystery of God was made manifest for the first time, even though in veiled form. The Fathers of the Church sang of her with lofty expressions. "You are splendor of light, O Mary, in the sublime spiritual kingdom! In you the Father, who is without beginning and whose power enveloped you, is glorified. In you the Son, whom you carried in your womb, is adored. In you the Holy Spirit, who brought about in you the birth of the great king, is celebrated. It is thanks to you, O full of grace, that the holy and consubstantial Trinity was made known to the world."[1]

She, the "Mother of the Son of God," the "beloved daughter of the Father," the "temple of the Holy Spirit"—Vatican II thus highlights the sublime relationships of Mary with the three divine persons[2]—is "full of the Trinity," therefore the image and model of the Church, of humanity divinized.

"Mary," Chiara writes, "Mother of beautiful Love,[3] had abundantly known . . . supernatural love. Born full of grace, she was overshadowed by Love in person—the Holy Spirit—when the Word became incarnate in her womb" and was then "covered by his flames at Pentecost."[4]

Therefore, the mother par excellence, the mother of God and our mother, "is an explanation of God, an open book that explains God: because God is love.

"The love in God was so great as to bring him to die the

most atrocious death for us—in order to save us. This is the purpose that impels a mother's love: the good and the safety of her child.

"Such is Mary: the creature who imitates God the most and who best shows him to us,"⁵ being herself what he most characteristically is: Love.

Chiara, referring back to a period of light in which the mystery of Mary was being revealed to her inside the mystery of love, which is God, explains:

> It seemed to us to have better understood how she loved the Father, how she was taught by the Son how to love the Father, and, as a consequence, how much she was loved by the Father. We felt as though we saw fully accomplished in her Jesus' prayer to the Father: "you loved them as you loved me" (Jn 17:23), because by the Father loved her as he loved the Son.
>
> We saw her therefore as *the daughter par excellence*, "the beloved daughter of the Father" (LG 53: F, 414).
>
> She was God's daughter as—but in a very different way—Jesus is God's Son. . . . And, as Jesus is the Son generated by the love of the Father, 'the Son that he loves' (Col 1:13, NJB), Mary, the daughter of God, was—as we came to call her—*the woman of love.*⁶

She is "the living, most pure and radiant image of God who is love, almost the incarnation of love or the arms of providence extended to humanity in order to save it, to dry tears, to close wounds, to point to the Eternal."⁷ In looking to her, therefore, in reliving her, we will complete the "magnificent journey" planned by God-Love for us: "from the Trinity to the Trinity."⁸

ABBREVIATIONS

In citing works in the notes, short titles have generally been used. Works frequently cited have been identified by the following abbreviations:

CC	*La Civiltà Cattolica.*
DES	*Dizionario Enciclopedico di Spiritualità.*
DS	Ed. Denzinger-Schonmetzer, *Enchiridion Symbolorum.* A collection of more important Church documents.
DV	*Dei verbum* (The dogmatic constitution on divine revelation).
EV	*Enchiridion Vaticanum.* Six volume collection of official Catholic documents in original languages plus Italian translation.
F	Austin Flannery, O.P., *Vatican II: Conciliar and Postconciliar Documents* (New York: Costello Publishing Co., 1986). Volume 1 of "Vatican Collection."
LG	*Lumen gentium* (The dogmatic constitution on the Church.)
NDT	*Nuovo Dizionario di Teologia.*
OR	*L'Osservatore Romano.* Vatican daily, published in Italian.
PG	J.P. Migne, *Patrologia Graeca.* Paris, 1857-1866.
PL	J.P. Migne, *Patrologia Latina.* Paris, 1844-1855.
REC	Recording.
SC	*Sources Chrétiennes,* edited by H. de Lubac and J. Danieloe, Paris.
Scr. Sp./1	Lubich, Chiara, *Scritti Spirituali/1. L'attrattiva del Tempo Moderno* (Spiritual writings/1. The attraction of modern times) (Rome: Città Nuova, 1978). A collection of three titles: *Meditazioni* (Meditations), Rome, 1959; *Pensieri* (Thoughts), Rome, 1961; and *Frammenti* (Fragments), Rome, 1963.

Scr. Sp./2	Lubich, Chiara, *Scritti Spirituali/2. L'essenziale di oggi* (Spiritual writings/2. What's essential today) (Rome: Città Nuova, 1978). A collection of two titles: *Saper Perdere* (Knowing how to lose), Rome, 1969; and *Sí, Sí, No, No* (Yes, yes, no, no), Rome, 1973.
Scr. Sp./3	Lubich, Chiara, *Scritti Spirituali/3. Tutti Uno* (Spiritual writings/3. All one) (Rome: Città Nuova, 1979). A collection of four titles: *Tutti Siano Uno* (That all may be one), Rome, 1968; *La Carità Come Ideale* (Charity as an ideal), Rome, 1971; *Parola di Vita* (The Word of life), Rome, 1975; and *Dove Due o Tre . . .* (Where two or three . . .), Rome, 1976.
ThQ	*Theologische Quartalschrift*.
WRIT	Unpublished writing.

NOTES

Preface and Introduction

1. Chiara Lubich is the founder and current president of the Focolare Movement or Work of Mary. She is a contemporary figure who is well known both in and outside of Church circles for her original and notable contribution of life and teaching, and who has been recognized on many occasions by Popes Paul VI and John Paul II.

Born in Trent, Italy on January 22, 1920, Chiara Lubich, in 1943, gave life to the Focolare, which received its first diocesan approval from Bishop Carlo de Ferrari in 1947, and the first pontifical approval from Pope John XXIII in 1962. The most recent approval of the Work of Mary and its General Statutes, which were updated and revised, came on June 29, 1990 with a *Decree* from the Holy See, in which, among other things, it states that the Focolare Movement has developed and spread "in faithfulness to its charism" and "has brought abundant spiritual fruits to the Church and a credible witness of unity to the world" (*General Statutes of the Work of Mary*, 4).

Chiara participated as an observer in the Extraordinary Synod of Bishops in 1985, and then in the Ordinary Synod in 1987, she delivered a talk on spiritualities and movements at a plenary session (*cf. Living City*, January 1988, 4-8).

Chiara has received various awards: the Templeton Prize for Progress in Religion on April 6, 1977, in London (cf. *Living City*, May/June 1977); the Plaque of St. Catherine, because—since she is a woman and layperson like St. Catherine, who was a Doctor of the Church—she has revealed and sparked the evangelical fire of Christ in the world, beyond any barrier of language, custom, ideology and religion (cf. *Living City*, February 1988, 2-5); and she has received notable recognitions in the ecumenical field: the cross of the Order of St. Augustine of Canterbury, presented on June 10, 1981, by the Primate of the Anglican Church of England, Robert Runcie (cf. *Living City*, December 1981, 4-7); a special gift of the Byzantine Cross, presented by the ecumenical Patriarch Dimitrios I on June 9, 1984, at Istanbul (cf. *Living City*, November 1984, 17-20); and on October 23, 1988, in Augsburg, Germany, the Festival of the Peace of Augsburg award for the "development of interconfessional relations," to which she gave a particular contribution through her profound spirituality and intense ecumenical activity (cf. *Living City*, January 1989, 9).

2. *Focolare* is an Italian word meaning "hearth" or "family fireside."

It was the name given to the Chiara and her first companions by others who felt the "warmth" of their love. Focolare refers to the movement as a whole, known also as the Work of Mary.

3. Cf. C. Lubich, "Sintesi della spiritualità," in *Mariapoli*, Rome, 1968, 73: "Just as a photograph whether it is taken from the front, the side or from above, can produce an image of a person so a sprirituality, while highlighting a particular aspect of Christianity, is Christianity, because it contains everything," and "To ask ourselves with each action we make: am I evangelizing?" in *Mariapolis*, 10-11 (1989): 7-8: "We can say that our spirituality undoubtedly rests on twelve points in the gospel which the Spirit underlined for us, but it is also true that our spirituality is the gospel."

4. Cf. C. Lubich, "La nostra storia. 40 anni fa il primo focolare," in *Città Nuova* 2 (1984): 37, and *May They All Be One* (New York, 1984), 27 (hereafter *All One*).

5. Cf. J. M. R. Tillard, "Le *sensus fidelium*: reflexion theologique," in *Foi populaire foi savante* (Paris, 1976), 9-40.

6. Cf. C. Vagaggini, *Teologia*, in NDT (Alba, 1977), 1695-96, and *Esperienza*, in DES (Rome, 1975), 720. The author cites a quotation from St. Anselm D'Aosta, who, among other things, writes: "Who does not believe does not understand, because the one who does not believe does not experience, and the one who does not experience does not know" (*De incarnatione Verbi* 1, in DES, 724).

7. C.T.I. (International Theological Commission), *L'interpretazione dei dogmi*, in CC 8 (1990): 169.

8. M. Schneider, *Unterscheidung der Geister* (Wien, 1981), 2-3, cited by G. Greshake in *Problemi e prospettive di teologia dogmatica* (Brescia, Italy, 1983), 301.

9. M. D. Chenu, *Le Saulchoir, una scuola di teologia* (Casale Monferrato, Italy, 1982), 59.

10. V. Lossky, *La teologia mistica della Chiesa d'Oriente* (Bologna, 1967), 4-5; P. Evdokimov, *L'amore folle di Dio* (Rome, 1981), 43.

11. C. Lubich, REC, "Reciprocal Love is the Fundamental Point of the Spirituality of Unity," to a group of bishops, Castelgandolfo, Italy, January 23, 1989.

Chapter 1. Like A Flash of Lightning—The Discovery that God Is Love

1. Cf. C. Lubich, "Dio è amore," *Colloqui con i Gen*, 4th ed. (Rome, 1979), 190, and *All One*, 27-28.

2. It was 1943, during the Second World War.

3. C. Lubich, WRIT, "God-Love and Charity in the Focolare Movement," to a group of bishops, Rocca di Papa, Italy, February 13, 1979.

4. C. Lubich, letter, June 1944, in *Gen* 6 (1968): 1.

5. C. Lubich, letter to Elena, June 7, 1944, in E. Robertson, *Chiara* (Ireland, 1978), 20-21.
6. C. Lubich, "Dio è amore," in *Colloqui con i Gen*, 190.
7. Cf. A. Latourelle, *Teologia della rivelazione*, 3d ed. (Assisi, 1970), 494-514. "The Holy Spirit . . . makes us penetrate the depths of the first revelation . . . renders it current for every generation . . . assures the continuity and the faithfulness of this growing penetration (ibid., 513).
8. C. Spicq, *Agape dans le Nouveau Testament* (Paris, 1959) 3:274, 321.
9. Cf. ibid., 322.
10. John Paul II, "God is love," homily, Grosseto, Italy, May 21, 1989, in *La Traccia* 5 (1989): 551.
11. W. Kasper, "Wer ist Jesus Christus fur uns heute? Zur gegenwärtigen Diskussion um die Gottessohnschaft Jesu," in ThQ 154 (1974): 217.
12. C. Lubich, "Dio è amore," in *Colloqui con i Gen*, 190.
13. Ibid., 192.; "Il Dio in cui credere," in *Città Nuova* 4 (1978): 41.
14. C. Lubich, *All One*, 27.
15. L. Scheffczyk, *Il Dio che verrà* (Turin, 1975), 98.
16. C. Lubich, *All One*, 25. *The General Statutes of the Work of Mary*, art. 8, states: "They strive therefore to love God-Love with all their heart, mind and strength (cf. Mt 22:37 and 1 Jn 4:16-18). They choose him as the ideal of their life."
17. The word Ideal has come to be used in the Focolare primarily to mean God, chosen as the one aim in life; it also stands for the Focolare spirituality and the way it is lived in daily life.
18. J. M. R. Tillard, "Le dynamisme des fondations," in *Vocation* 295 (1981): 23.
19. Cf. K. Rahner, *L'elemento dinamico nella Chiesa* (Brescia, 1970), 41-78.
Recently, Cardinal J. Ratzinger, in referring to the new ecclesial movements and in particular to the Focolare Movement, said that in them there can be seen "a new generation inspired by the profound rediscovery of the authentic faith of the Church," "a new intelligence of faith, capable of interpreting it and of celebrating it in a new way" (cf. G. Boselli, "Ratzinger ai Focolari," in *Città Nuova* 1 [1990]: 42).

Chapter 2. Because God Is Love, He Is a Father

1. Cf. C. Lubich, "Dio è amore," in *Coloqui con i Gen*, 190, and "Spiritualities and Movements," in *Living City*, January 1988, 4.
2. C. Lubich, "Ora tutto è nuovo," in *Città Nuova* 23 (1988): 11.
3. C. Lubich, *Diary 1964/65* (New York, 1987), 72-73.
4. Cf. J. Jeremias, *Abba* (Brescia, 1968), 66., and *Teologia del Nuovo Testamento* (Brescia, 1972), 76.

5. C. Lubich, "Abba Padre!" in *Mariapoli* 3 (1989): 2-3.

6. On various occasions Chiara has spoken wonderfully on this mystery. "I find in myself" she said recently, "an always deeper understanding of him. . . . 'In the beginning was the Word.' The Father created looking at him: he was the model, he was the design . . ." "Heaven will be in the bosom of the Father, it will be inside the Father. Moreover, our heaven will be the Word, from where we came as a design, and in this design, which is the Word of God, we will return" (C. Lubich, REC, to the Focolarini, Hyde Park, New York, May 18 and 20, 1990).

7. The Fathers expressed the awareness that the Church had of this reality since the early centuries. Leo the Great writes, "The mystery of this grace is very great. This gift, that is, that God makes the human person his son and that the human person calls God 'Father,' surpasses all gifts" (*Serm.* 26, *De nativ. Dom.* 6, 4: PL 54:214).

8. L. Bouyer, *Il Padre invisibile* (Rome, 1979), 202, 195.

It is this reality, to which the infinite love of God elevates humankind, that Maximus the Confessor contemplates and describes as follows: "If it is for this that the son of God and of the Father, God-Word, became the son of man and man, that is, in order to make men and women gods and sons of God, we believe that we will be able to find ourselves there where Christ himself is now found with our own condition as head of the entire body, having become for us our forerunner in company with the Father (cf. Col 1:18; Heb 6:20). In fact, in the assembly of the gods, that is, of those who are saved, God will be present in their midst (cf. Ps 81:1), distributing the allotted shares of that happiness without establishing any distance from those who are worthy of them" (*Seconda centuria* 25: PG 90:1136).

9. Cf. C. Lubich, "Dio è amore," in *Colloqui con i Gen*, 191.

10. C. Lubich, WRIT, Chiara's diary, Rocca di Papa, Italy, January 13, 1979.

11. C. Lubich, "Spiritualities and Movements," in *Living City*, January 1988, 4-8.

12. C. Lubich, WRIT, Chiara's diary, Rocca di Papa, Italy, February 4, 1968.

13. *The General Statutes of the Work of Mary*, art. 23.

14. John Paul II, *Dives in misericordia* (On the mercy of God) 7, November 30, 1980 (Boston: Daughters of St. Paul, 1980), 26. With a fine intuition, De Margerie shows that, after the first revelation which God makes to Moses about his name: "I am who am" (Ex 3:14), a second follows, in which he seems to define his being by proclaiming himself "a merciful and gracious God, slow to anger and rich in kindness and fidelity" (Ex 34:6); (cf. *Les perfections du Dieu de Jesus Christ* [Paris, France 1981], 257).

15. These various aspects of the merciful love of God are all expressed in the figure of the father in Luke's well-known parable. Theologians are in accord in holding that the parable of the prodigal son could be better named as the parable of the merciful Father. It is here where, as Scheffzyck affirms, "the revelation of God in the New Testament—in its entirety—finds its focal point, the center of its fullest concretization" (*Il Dio che verrà*, 78).

16. C. Lubich, *When Our Love Is Charity* (New York, 1991), 134, and "Un amore che crea," in *Città Nuova* 24 (1984): 10-11.

17. C. Lubich, *Meditations* (New York, 1986), 54-55.

18. Maximus the Confessor, *Mystag.* 24: PG 91:713.

Chapter 3. Responding to God-Love by Being Love

1. C. Lubich, "La spiritualità del Movimento dei Focolari," in *Mariapoli* 11 (1984): 3, and *All One*, 29.

2. C. Lubich, *Il Dio in cui credere*.

3. C. Lubich, *Diary 1964/65*, 142.

4. Chiara explains this relationship that was sparked and is sustained through faith in love: "To believe in God-Love, to believe in the love of the Father, of the Son and of the Holy Spirit for us. To believe also in Mary's love for us, a love that is an expression, a manifestation of God's love" ("Tutto tuo," in *Mariapoli* 6 [1988]: 2).

5. C. Lubich, "Dio è amore," in *Colloqui con i Gen*, 191.

6. Cf. Paul VI, "Il patrocinio di Maria sulla Pentecoste perenne," in *Insegnamenti di Paolo VI* (1969) 7: 687.

7. Cf. C. Lubich, "Il bambino evangelico," in *Città Nuova* 23 (1990): 8-9.

8. C. Lubich, WRIT, Chiara's diary, February 27, 1967.

9. Cf. C. Lubich, WRIT, Chiara's diary, June 17 and 20, 1973.

10. C. Lubich, REC, to the Focolarine, Rocca di Papa, Italy, December 6, 1973.

11. C. Lubich, "Liberi di amare," in *Città Nuova* 17 (1987): 11.

12. C. Lubich, "Il sogno di quel bambino," in *Città Nuova* 23 (1985): 10-11.

13. C. Lubich, "Per una civiltà dell'unità," in *Città Nuova* 12 (1988): 34.

14. C. Lubich, *All One*, 29.

15. C. Lubich, letter to Elena, April 16, 1944; cf. *Detti Gen* (Rome, 1977), 67.

16. C. Lubich, "Essere fuoco," in *Mariapoli* (1989), 3. Since the beginning of the Focolare, in fact, the choice of God-Love was immediately translated into the "choice of the way of love" (cf. *Unity and Jesus Forsaken* [New York, 1985], 87).

John Paul II, in a talk given at the conclusion of his visit to the

International Center of the Focolare Movement on August 19, 1984, noted at length that, for its members, love is the "inspiring spark" of all that they are and all that they do in the world, "the fundamental nucleus" of their life, "their charism." And placing it alongside the "many radicalisms of love," which, arising from the "supreme radicalism of Christ Jesus," have adorned the history of the Church—as those of St. Francis, St. Ignatius, Charles de Foucauld—the "evangelical radicalism of love of Chiara, of the Focolarini," has recognized its particular impact in the life of today's society and its intrinsic force in "giving witness to God who is love." "*God is love,*" he continued to explain: "This means that when love is lived, when love is made victorious, then God is made visible" (cf. John Paul II, "Al Movimento dei Focolari: 'Colmate il vuoto d'amore del mondo,' " in *Insegnamenti di Giovanni Paolo II* [1984] 7/2: 223-225).

These words of the pope revived in Chiara the memory of an important moment of her life, when, as a young girl fascinated by her new Ideal, her father asked her, "But, my daughter, what is this Ideal?" She responded, "It is love, Papa. It is love."

It was the clear, immediate, and decisive commitment, flowing from the rediscovery of God-Love and of her own divine kinship, to love him in return, to love everyone. This supernatural love is the soul of the Focolare and—as was mentioned—since the very beginning was highlighed in its rich and original spirituality, which rests on the principal truths of faith and is defined as the spirituality of unity.

17. C. Lubich, *Yes Yes, No No* (London, 1977), 50.

18. Cf. C. Lubich, *Meditations*, 78-79: "Love," Chiara writes, "is the essence of God, the life itself of the children of God, the breath of the Christian" (10-11).

19. C. Lubich, Scr. Sp./1, 261.

20. C. Lubich, *Dio Amore e la carità nel Movimento dei Focolari*.

21. Cf. C. Lubich, *Meditations*, 38, and *On the Holy Journey* (New York, 1988), 89: "Love gives us our being. . . . In all the moments in which we do not love, we no longer are, we do not exist."

22. C. Lubich, REC, "Comments on the Statutes," Grottaferrata, Italy, June 3, 1967; cf. *Knowing How To Lose* (London, 1981) 61.

23. Gregory of Nyssa says: "God is thus love and the source of love. . . . The creator has also imprinted in us this character. 'This is how all will know you for my disciples: your love for one another' (Jn 13:35). Therefore, if this is not prevalent, the entire image becomes disfigured" (*De hom. op.* 5: PG 44:137).

24. C. Spicq, *Agape dans le Nouveau Testament*, 277-78.

25. Maximus the Confessor, cited in "Un Monaco Contemplativo," in *Dio amore ci dona la deificazione* (Rome, 1990), 19, and *Ep. 43 ad Joan. cub.*: PG 91:640. Also Athanasius underlines that our divinization is freely given: "One alone" he affirms, "is the Son by nature.

We become equally sons, not however as he by nature, but by grace; we are human beings called gods, not as the true God and his Son, but in the way God wanted by granting us this grace" (*De Incarn.* 54: PG 25:192).

Chapter 4. Because God Is Love, He Is Trinity

1. Agape is a Greek term that the New Testament—as is known—had adopted in order to express the new and rich content of Christian love. Thus it has signified, since then, a love that is a gift, a gift of self.

2. C. Spicq, *Agape dans Nouveau testament*, 323-24.

3. Therefore, as W. Kasper says, the scriptural announcement "God is love" is, at the same time, an ontological announcement, that is, which reveals the being most proper to God, and, in regards to the human person, is a salvific announcement: "Only because he is love, can God reveal himself and share himself with us as love" (*Il Dio di Gesù Cristo* [Brescia, 1984], 330).

4. W. Kasper, 410, 411. "In the intimacy of trinitarian life," M. Bordoni writes, "the Spirit is the *personal end* in which the reciprocal love of the Father and of the Son is self-transcended; it is personally, therefore, the ecstasy of such a love that, precisely in the ecstasy as such, remains immanent in itself" (*Gesù di Nazaret Signore e Cristo* [Rome, 1986] 3: 519).

5. A. Ganoczy, *Dio grazia per il mondo* (Brescia, 1988), 96. "A similar mystery," the author explains, "cannot be other than the mystery of *persons*," if, for us creatures, " 'being a person' means to have the *capability of entering into free relationships joined with an absolute respect of the dignity* of the other. Understood in this way, the individuality of each is not dissolved in the communion, but becomes a carrier of an affirmed personality" (p. 268-69), accomplished, that is, in the communion itself, in the gift of self.

6. Augustine, *De Trinitate* VIII, 8, 12: PL 42:958; VIII, 10, 14: PL 42:960; VI, 5, 7: PL 42:928.

7. C. Spicq underlines the importance of the word "as" (in Greek *kathos*, which means of the same nature), which expresses the identity of the love of the Father for Jesus and of Jesus for the disciples. In his evocative research, the author explains that the Greek conjunction *kathos* is stronger than the others (*os, osper, oste,* etc.), which also mean "as," and, among other things, he observes:

"The love of Christ for his people is analogous to the love that the Father has for him; it is of the same nature, therefore divine." Furthermore, "the essential words of the precept (the reciprocal love that Jesus speaks about to the disciples), the words that specify this love, are 'as I have loved you' (Jn 15:12)." Certainly among them it is not a question of a love of the same intensity and of the same sanctity of that of Jesus, but "of a love of the same quality and of the same nature.... *Kathos* does not indicate a simple comparison, an analogy that is more or less distant or a superficial similarity... but a deep conformity, for the example of Jesus is also the norm of love and its foundation" (*Agape dans le Nouveau Testament*, 161-74). And, in a note, he affirms: "In 'his departing words' (Jn 13:17) '*kathos*' has a strong theological meaning: imitation and similarity, extension and assimilation: *as* the Father loves Jesus, so Jesus loves the believers (cf. Jn 15:9; 17:23) and the believers must love one another with the same love (cf. Jn 15:12)... *as* the Father and the Son are one, the disciples must be one (cf. Jn 17:21)" (173, n. 1).

8. C. Lubich, "Il comandamento 'nuovo,' " in *Città Nuova* 8 (1980): 41.

9. R. Latourelle, *Teologia della rivelazione*, 512-13.

10. C. Lubich, "Unità e comunità" and "La comunità cristiana," in *Fides*, October 1948, 4.

11. Interview of Chiara Lubich on Italian television (April 17, 1978).

12. H. Mühlen, *Una mystica persona* (Rome, 1968), 480-81. The Orthodox theology, on its part, has always retained that, to know the mystery of God one and triune, one must enter into an intimate communion with him. Trinitarian theology, therefore, is a theology of union, as Evdokimov affirms in the passage cited above, which we will now present here in its entirety. "Theology is mystical life and mystical life is theology, and even more it is the apex of theology, theology par excellence, contemplation of the Trinity" (cf. Introduction, note 9 above).

13. C. Lubich, letter, May 11, 1948, in J. Povilus, *Gesù in mezzo nel pensiero di Chiara Lubich* (Rome, 1981), 71 (hereafter *Gesù in mezzo*).

14. C. Lubich, "L'unità," December 2 and 12, 1946, in Povilus, *Gesù in mezzo*, 11-12, 67.

15. C. Lubich, WRIT, 1949, in Povilus, *Gesù in mezzo*, 69.

16. C. Lubich, WRIT, March 27, 1950, in Povilus, *Gesù in mezzo*, 72.

17. Cf. B. De Margerie, *La Trinité chrétienne dans l'histoire* (Paris, 1975), 244-54.

18. Cf. Jn 10:38; 14, 9-10; 17, 21.

19. Cf. for example, Athanasius, *De decretis nicaenae synodis* 26: PG, 26:461-66; Irenaeus of Lyons, *Adv. Haer.* 3, 6, 2: SC: 211:68-71; Gregory Nazianzen, Ep 101, 6: SC 208:38, who applies the concept of perichoresis also to the relationship of the two natures in Christ.

20. John Damascene, *De fide orthodoxa* I, 14: PG 94:860.

21. Fulgentius of Ruspe, *De fide liber ad Petrum* 1, 4: PL 65:674. In reality, the different emphasis given in the Greek and in the Latin context to the concept of perichoresis is reflected also in the Latin trinitarian doctrine itself, as it testifies to the different translation of

the term *circumsessio* (and *circumincessio*) or *circuminsessio*, the first having a more dynamic meaning, the second more static.

22. Circumincession is the mystery of the sacred indwelling of the three divine persons with one another.

23. Cf. DS 1331.

24. Gregory of Nazianzen, *In sanctum baptisma* 40, 41: PG 36:417.

25. B. De Margerie, *La Trinité chrétienne*..., 246.

26. Cf. Document of the International Theological Commission, "Alcune questioni reguardanti la cristologia," which states that "the Son's distancing himself from the Father in his emptying of self (*kenosis*)" (cf. Phil 2:7) and in the experience of the abandonment he lived (cf. Mt 27:46) is "his own part, in the economy of the redemption, of the (utmost) distinction of the persons of the Holy Trinity, who are perfectly united in the identity of a same nature and of an infinite love" (IV D 8, in CC 21 [1980]: 276, Ital. trans. with adaptations; cf. original Latin text in EV 7:683).

27. C. Lubich, WRIT, July 25, 1949, in Povilus, *Gesù in mezzo*, 75.

28. "Love," S. Bulgakov explains, "finds itself in the other, and exists only in the self-identification with the other; in itself it is as if it does not exist; all the same, in this non-existing there is all the power of its existence, in the measure in which the other exists for the first and the life unfolds in the other." And, in penetrating the kenotic dimension of love inside the life of the Trinity, he reveals that "the trinitarian self-revelation in the divine life comprises two inseparably joined acts . . . death and resurrection. . . . Two forms of love: immolation and its triumph, 'perfect joy': the Father who exhausts himself in the birth (in generating) the Son . . . the Son . . . who exhausts himself in becoming born; in all this and beyond, the vivifying Spirit, the breath of divine love in all its fullness, in its triumph" (*Il Paraclito* [Bologna, 1971], 396, 288).

29. C. Lubich, WRIT, September 2, 1949, in Povilus, *Gesù in mezzo*, 75; cf. Scr. Sp./1, 140.

30. C. Lubich, WRIT, 1950, in Povilus, *Gesù in mezzo*, 77.

31. W. Kasper, *Il Dio di Gesù Cristo*, 410.

32. C. Lubich, "Cristo nella comunità," in *Città Nuova* 11 (1978), 40.

33. C. Lubich, WRIT, November 6, 1949, in Povilus, *Gesù in mezzo*, 73.

34. C. Lubich, WRIT, Chiara's diary, May 22, 1972.

35. C. Lubich, WRIT, Chiara's diary, June 8, 1972. Chiara, having been invited to speak in Tokyo to 12,000 Buddhists about her experience of Christian faith, was able not only to communicate her discovery of God-Love, of his paternity, but she was also able to explain the profound unity that a Christian, guided by the Spirit of God, can find with Christ, sharing in his filial relationship with the

Father, to the extent of penetrating, in a certain way, the mystery of God who, because he is love, is Trinity and Unity (cf. *Incontri con l'Oriente* [Rome, 1986], 24-25).

36. Cf. R. Moretti, "L'inabitazione trinitaria," in *La mistica* (Rome, 1984) 2: 115-16. Augustine explains a specification concerning this trinitarian presence: "God is present everywhere with his divinity, but he is not everywhere with the grace of indwelling. It is by means of this indwelling—in which there is the indubitable recognition of his love that is freely given that, instead of saying: 'Our Father who is everywhere . . .' we say: 'Our Father who is in heaven,' in order to recall in prayer that he is the temple we must become; in as much as we are, we will be a part of his communion and a part of the family of his adopted sons" (*Ep. 187 ad Dardanum* 5, 16: PL 33:838).

37. Bernard of Clairvaux, *Sermon 71 in Cant. 6, 10*: PL 183:1126.
38. C. Lubich, *All One*, 52.
39. Ibid.
40. C. Lubich, "Risurrezione di Roma," in *La Via* (October 29, 1949), 5; cf. *Yes Yes, No No*, 69-72.
41. C. Lubich, Scr. Sp./2, 144.
42. Cf. C. Lubich, *Sintesi della spiritualità*, 76: "It is the life of the Most Holy Trinity," Chiara will say to a large ecumenical group, "that we must try to imitate, by loving one another, with the grace of God, as the persons of the Most Holy Trinity love one another. But it is truly this life that is the strongest witness of God in the world."
43. C. Lubich, letter, May 11, 1948, in Povilus, *Gesù in mezzo*, 71.
44. Cyprian, *De orat. domin.*, 23, in LG 4: F, 352.
45. Origen, *Exegetica in Psalmos*, 23: PG 12:1266.
46. Cf. H. De Lubac, *Meditazioni sulla Chiesa* (Milan, 1965), 293; Y. Congar, "Implicazioni cristologiche e pneumatologiche dell'ecclesiologia del Vaticano II," in *L'ecclesiologia del Vaticano II: dinamismi e prospettive* (Bologna, 1981), 108.
47. C. Lubich, "Woman: Catalyst of Peace and Unity," in *Living City*, September 1989, 4; cf. *When Our Love Is Charity*, 87-89.
48. Cf. John Paul II, "Il Vangelo è vita per le anime e per l'intera società." To the participants at the international congress of the New Humanity Movement, in *Insegnamenti di Giovanni Paolo II* (1983) 6/1: 778.

Chapter 5. Trinitarian Love in the Workings of the Three Divine Persons

1. C. Lubich, *Meditations*, 101.
2. C. Lubich, "Tutto è di Dio," in *Colloqui con i Gen*, 130.
3. C. Lubich, Scr. Sp./1, 204.
4. It is the affirmation of the Fourth Lateran Council (1215), DS 804.

Later on the Council of Florence (1442) will specify that the Father, the Son and the Spirit are not three origins, but one single origin of creation, cf. DS 1331. The testimony of the Fathers is also very significant. Fulgentius of Ruspe writes: "All the realities in the heavens and on earth, visible and invisible . . . are the work and creation of the Holy Trinity; this is the one God, Creator and Lord of all things, who is eternal, omnipotent, and good" (*De fide liber ad Petrum*, III, 25: PL 65:683). And, among the Doctors of the Church, there is St. Thomas: "Creation . . . is the common work of the entire Trinity" (*Summa Theologiae* I, q. 45, a.6, ad c).

5. Augustine, *In Jo.* 20, 9: PL 35:1561.

6. H. U. von Balthasar, "Le Saint-Esprit l'inconnu au dela' du Verbe," in *Lumiere et Vie* 67 (1964): 122.

7. C. Lubich, "L'immensità di Dio," in *Mariapoli* 1 (1987), 9.

8. C. Lubich, REC, Vigo di Fassa, Italy, August 19, 1955.

9. C. Lubich, Scr. Sp./2, 140-41; cf. Francis of Assisi, "Il cantico delle creature," in *Fonti Francescane* (Assisi, 1977) 1: 178. Ambrose expresses the unity that underlies and links all things in the universe in the following way: "Who has not marvelled that the world, in its great variety as it is composed of different parts, could form a unitarian organism and that many different beings could have been able, through an indissoluble law of agreement and love, form a solid unity and a tight contexture, so much so that things of a completely different nature are knotted by a bond of harmony and peace, as though they were inseparable? . . . Yet, the divine power, incomprehensible to the human spirit and inexpressible in human terms, by its own desire, gave order to all these things" (*Hexameron*, dies II, serm. III, 1, 1: PL 14:144-45).

10. T. Spidlik, "La Trinità nella spiritualità della Chiesa Orientale," in *Il mistero del Dio vivente* (Rome, 1968), 243.

11. C. Lubich, *Meditations*, 69-71, 102-03.

12. C. Lubich, *Yes Yes, No No*, 37-44.

13. C. Lubich, "Cristo dispiegato nei secoli," in *La Rete* (April 1957), 8.

14. C. Lubich, *Meditations*, 52; Scr. Sp./1, 260-61.

15. C. Lubich, "Gesù è la Via," in *Gen* 8-9-10 (1989), insert p. 3.

16. C. Lubich, "La Legge di Loppiano," in *Gen* 7-8 (1982): 4.

17. Cf. C. Lubich, *Yes Yes, No No*, 145.

18. Cf. C. Lubich, *Meditations*, 25. "God, because he is love," Schurmann writes, "is so much a gift as to be capable of 'emptying' himself, of 'lowering himself' (cf. Phil 2:6.) to the measure of the incarnation, and even more, to the measure of death and of the hell of our sins, wherein the Father 'sacrifices' the Son in the abandonment of God and the Son 'gives' himself to the Father in the midst of this same abandonment" (*Gesù di fronte alla propria morte* [Brescia, 1983], 177-78).

19. Cf. H. U. von Balthasar, *Cordula ovverosia il caso serio*, 3d ed. (Brescia, 1969), 30.

20. Chiara, in the following way, explains the intimate relationship between the abandonment of Jesus and the handing over to the Father of the bond of love that united him to the Father—the Holy Spirit—so that men and women could also share the same Spirit. "We can perhaps think . . . that this particular pain of Jesus, his being forsaken, has a special relationship with the Holy Spirit. And this is for the simple reason that when we give something away we have to feel its loss. On the cross Jesus felt, at that tremendous moment, his detachment from the Father. But who bonded him and still bonds him to the Father in a personal communion, if not the Holy Spirit himself?" If in the passage of Christ to the Father—as a theologian holds—"the most perfect realization of the human love of the Word incarnate is accomplished, the sign of the breath of love from which the Spirit proceeds," since the abandonment is the supreme expression of Christ's love, "it is in that cry where lies 'the most perfect realization of the human love of the Word incarnate' . . . it is in the abandonment where lies 'the sign of the breath of love from which proceeds the Holy Spirit' " (*Unity and Jesus Forsaken*, 75-76; cf. M. Bordoni, *Il tempo: valore filosofico e mistero teologico* [Rome, 1965], 141-42).

21. C.T.I. (International Theological Commission), *Teologia-Cristologia-Antropologia*, I C 3: EV 8:427.

22. H. U. von Balthasar, *Teodrammatica* (Milan, 1986) 4: 302-03.

23. *Unity and Jesus Forsaken*, 51-52.

24. Ibid., 49.

25. Ibid., 70-71.

26. C. Lubich, letter, perhaps of 1944, in *Diary 1964/65*, 150.

27. *Unity and Jesus Forsaken*, 71.

28. This is the purpose of the redeeming Incarnation, according to the constant teaching of the Fathers: "The Word of God . . . by his immense charity made himself what we are in order to make us what he is" (Irenaeus, *Adv. Haer.* 5, Praef.: PG 7:1120); "(God) became man in order to deify us in him" (Athanasius, *Ad Adelph.* 4: PG 26:1077).

29. John Paul II, "The Holy Spirit, love of the Father and of the Son," in *L'Osservatore Romano*, November 15, 1990, 4. The attribution, love, given to the Holy Spirit as his own name is constant throughout the Fathers and the Doctors of the Church, while still affirming that love is the very essence of God, therefore common to all three of the divine persons. Augustine says: "Just as we specifically call the one Word of God with the name 'wisdom,' so too, in a general way, also the Spirit is specifically called by the name 'charity,' even though the Father and the Son are, in a general way, also charity" (*De Trinitate* XV, 17, 31: PL 42, 1082).

30. Cf. C. Lubich, *On The Holy Journey*, 52-53.

31. C. Lubich, *Diario 1964/65*, 131; cf. *Knowing How To Lose*, 82.
32. Basil writes: "Just as clear and transparent bodies, when penetrated by light, also become resplendent themselves and in their turn sources of light, so too souls who are carriers of the Spirit and are illuminated by the Spirit, in their turn become spiritual and pour out grace onto others. Here lies the intelligence of the mysteries, the heavenly conversation . . . here begins perennial joy, permanence in God, resemblance with God, here is where—and nothing more sublime could be desired—we become God" (*De Spir. S.* 9, 23: PG 32:109).
33. William of Saint Thierry, "Lettera d'oro," n. 263, in M. J. Le Guillou, *Il mistero del Padre* [Milan, Italy, 1979], 109).
34. C. Lubich, "Mossi dallo Spirito," in *Città Nuova* 10 (1985): 10, and "Lo Spirito Santo per noi," in *Gen* 4 (1981): 3.
35. C. Lubich, REC, to the Focolarini in Montet, Switzerland, August 3, 1989, and *On The Holy Journey*, 75-77.
36. John of the Cross had affirmed this in the soul that is divinely transformed, and which "enacts in God the same spiration of love that the Father breathes in the Son and the Son in the Father, which is the Holy Spirit himself" (*Spiritual Canticle*, red. A. str. 38, 2, in *Opere*, 4th ed. [Rome, 1979], 959).
37. D. Mollat, *Giovanni maestro spirituale* (Rome, 1980), 67.

Mary—The Radiant Image of God Who Is Love

1. Gregory il Taumaturgo, *Hom. 2 in Annuntiat. Virg. Mariae*: PG 10:1169. Cf. Andrew of Crete, *In Annuntiat. B. Mariae*: PG 97:909.
2. LG 53: F, 414.
3. Sir 24, 24, in "Vg iuxta LXX."
4. C. Lubich, "La famiglia e Maria," in *Città Nuova* 8 (1984): 30.
4. C. Lubich, "La città di Maria," in *Gen* 5 (1972): 1.
6. C. Lubich, REC, "Mary in the Experience of the Focolare Movement," to an ecumenical meeting of bishops associated with the Focolare Movement, Castelgandolfo, November 23, 1987.
7. C. Lubich, *Meditations*, 131.
8. C. Lubich, *A Call To Love* (New York, 1989), 163.

Works by Chiara Lubich Available in English

A CALL TO LOVE

Spiritual Writings, Vol. 1

"Chiara Lubich has established herself as a Christian writer of considerable proportions. Given her prolific literary output it is fitting that New City Press should issue a retrospective series of Lubich's best works, titled Spiritual Writings. The first work in this series *A Call to Love* comprises three of her most popular studies of momentous Christian living: *Our Yes to God* (1980), *The Word of Life* (1974), and *The Eucharist* (1977)."

B.C. Catholic

ISBN 0-911782-70-2, paper, 5 1/8 x 8, 180 pp.

WHEN OUR LOVE IS CHARITY

Spiritual Writings, Vol. 2

Since publishing her first book in 1959, Chiara Lubich has written extensively on a variety of spiritual topics drawn from the gospel message of unity. This second volume of spiritual writings binds together three of her previous works: *Charity, Jesus in Our Midst*, and *When Did We See You, Lord?*

ISBN 0-911782-93-1, paper, 5 1/8 x 8, 152 pp.

UNITY AND JESUS FORSAKEN

"Without being simplistic or reductionistic, Lubich challenges [the reader] to focus on Jesus forsaken as the

model for unity and the key to living a life of joy. . . . Lubich's essays reflect a balanced spirituality."
    Bishop Robert Morneau, Emmanuel Magazine
ISBN 0-911782-53-2, paper, 5 1/8 x 8, 105 pp.

FROM SCRIPTURE TO LIFE

"Contains commentaries that author Chiara Lubich has written on 12 different 'Words of Life.' Each section of the book includes true stories of people who applied the teaching of the Scripture passage."
    Catholic News Service

ISBN 0-911782-83-4, paper, 5 1/8 x 8, 112 pp.

MEDITATIONS

"[A] collection of brief but intensely meaningful thoughts carefully mined from the scriptures. Chiara helps us to see all the events of our lives as opportunities for our ultimate . . . perfection."
    Liguorian

ISBN 0-911782-20-6, paper 5 1/8 x 8, 134 pp.

ON THE HOLY JOURNEY

"Every two weeks, Chiara Lubich, foundress and president of the Focolare movement, sends out a spiritual message to committed members throughout the world. This is a collection of those meditations, the principal focus of which is a call to live out the 'holy journey' toward Christian perfection in the world by 'walking together' in the love of Jesus and Mary."
    Spiritual Book News

ISBN 0-911782-60-5, paper, 5 1/8 x 8, 166 pp.

DIARY 1964/65

"Add Chiara Lubich's name to the list of extraordinary Catholic women.... In 1964 and 1965 Chiara Lubich made several trips to North and South America to encourage the Focolarini who were establishing their work in the U.S., Argentina, and Brazil. Lubich's diary records her experiences and thoughts during these journeys."
New Oxford Review

ISBN 0-911782-55-9, paper, 5 1/8 x 8, 188 pp.

***Works on Chiara Lubich
and the Focolare Movement***

UNITY—OUR ADVENTURE

The Focolare Movement

This publication tells the story of an adventure: that of the Focolare movement. The book intends to offer a quick panorama of the Focolare's spirituality and history. It contains 40 color and 47 black and white photos.
ISBN 0-911782-56-7, cloth, 8 1/2 x 11, 80 pp.

STARS AND TEARS

by Michel Pochet

Through a series of interviews with Chiara Lubich, the author traces the development and the spirituality of the Focolare. The style and format is accessible to everyone.
ISBN 0-911782-54-0, paper, 5 1/8 x 8, 153 pp.

UNITED IN HIS NAME

Jesus in Our Midst in the Writings of Chiara Lubich
by Judith Povilus

A spiritual-dogmatic study that delves into some of the thoughts of Chiara Lubich on the presence of Christ in the community as seen in Matthew 18:20.
ISBN 1-56548-003-1, paper, 5 3/8 x 8 1/2, 136 pp.